To My friend and ~ ~~ ~~

Bob Prima.

Blessings my friend,

Christian Tantric Meditation Guide

David J. Miller

DEDICATION

To my Father

Dale Emerson Miller

CONTENTS

Acknowledgments   i

Preface   1

Introduction   4

Key Concepts   7

Introductory Practice: Grounding and Mindfulness   15

Stage One: Self Emptying   24

Stage Two: Divine Communion   42

Stage Three: Outreach Compassion   56

Meditation and Balance   85

Tantric Practice and Christian Tradition   89

Conclusion   93

Testimonial: The Author's Meditative Journey   94

References   100

ACKNOWLEDGMENTS

I am grateful to my wife Stacey and to my children for their love and support throughout this journey we call life.

I would like to acknowledge the contributions and support of Bruce Alderman, Buddhism and Integral Scholar, and Rev. Lou Kavar PhD, Psychology Instructor and Spiritual Director

I would also like to acknowledge the editorial contributions from my good friends Robert and Corey Armstrong.

PREFACE

This preface provides a brief description of some of my experiences in Christian Ministry and secular counseling that led to the creation of this book. A more detailed description of my meditative journey is provided in the "Testimonial" chapter toward the end of the book. In order to help explain how and why Tantric methods apply to this practice, a brief definition and history of Buddhist Tantric practice is also provided. Finally, some thoughts regarding compassion and whether being a "Christian" is a prerequisite for engaging in this practice are discussed.

As a child, I came to know Jesus the Christ as the embodiment of God's unconditional love toward humanity. My studies and experiences in Christianity, Buddhism, and other cultures and philosophies have served to strengthen my relationship with and understanding of Christ in those terms.

As an adult, through medical circumstances beyond my control, I found myself without a voice for several years. During this timeframe I also received my Master's in Theological Studies and practiced chaplain ministry in a homeless shelter setting. Having no voice, I was forced to "just listen" to the people I worked with, offering no advice whatever. I was blessed to witness not only the amazing stories and wonderful cultural diversity of the people I worked with, but also the miraculous healing properties that empathetic listening can provide. This experience led me to a deeper exploration of the power of listening, to myself, to God, and to others, through meditation.

Eventually I received my Master's in Community Counseling and began to share the practices I learned with clients in secular therapeutic settings. My explorations into mindfulness oriented meditation techniques and cognitive behavior therapy, combined with my Christian Ministry training and experience, eventually led to the development of this Christian Tantric Meditation practice.

Tantra originated in the Hindu tradition. The word Tantra is built from Sanskrit words meaning "elaborating on profound matters" and "liberation" (Wallis, 2012). One might define Tantra as a refined practice that develops insight for the purpose of illuminating a path to freedom.

Buddhism is often described in terms of "turns", or eras in which emphasis within teachings and writings have evolved. The first "turn" originated with Gautama Buddha himself, who described methods for dealing with and finding liberation from suffering that is part of the human condition. A good source for learning about the life and teachings of Buddha is "A Life of the Buddha" (Kohn, 2011).

The second turn of Buddhism included an emphasis on unconditional love and compassion towards all of humanity, who share the conditions of suffering in common. The philosophy associated with the second turn is known as Mahayana. A good source for learning about Mahayana philosophy is "The Way of Bodhisattva" (Padmakara, 2007).

The third turn of Buddhism incorporated Tantric teachings and practice from Hinduism. Tantric practice uses meditation to increase one's understanding of self and relationship with Divinity. One particular tantric practice is called Guru Yoga, which involves communing with Divinity. The philosophy associated with the third turn is known as Vajrayana. A good source for learning more about Buddhist Tantric philosophy and practice is "Introduction to Tantra" by Lama Yeshe (Yeshe, 2001).

With all of that said, Christian Tantric Meditation utilizes the Tantric meditation practices of self emptying, communing with Divinity, and sharing Compassion, from a Christian perspective. The Christian perspective informs us about who we are as humans made in the image of God. The Christian perspective recognizes Jesus the Christ as the person through whom we connect with God. The Christian perspective also motivates us to have compassion for ourselves and for others.

In recent years, in both Christianity and in Buddhism, a renewed emphasis has been placed on unconditional love and compassion. Both Pope Francis and the Dalai Lama have called a great deal of attention to sharing unconditional love and compassion with our fellow human beings. I hope that this will continue, and that other faith traditions will also emphasize their own roots in unconditional love and compassion.

The question has been asked whether "being a Christian" is required for learning Christian Tantric Meditation. From the traditional evangelical perspective, "accepting Christ as your personal Lord and Savior" is not a prerequisite. The only requirements are an openness to the possibility of communing with unconditionally loving Divinity, and the desire to be a more compassionate person.

While the name of Jesus the Christ identifies our immanent connection with Divinity, the four gospels and Judeo-Christian scripture bear witness to people experiencing Divinity in different ways and from different perspectives. I hope that practitioners learn to let go of preconceived ideas regarding "who Jesus is" and develop authentic relationships with unconditionally loving Divinity.

INTRODUCTION

Imagine sitting in an open field in the middle of a clear moonless night. Imagine seeing a vast panorama of stars from horizon to horizon. Now think about the burdens of life – including money, family, job stresses and anxieties and depressions we don't even know the source of. As we feel the weight of these forces, the beautiful and awe inspiring view fades until we no longer notice it at all.

Now imagine being in the same field, but this time with a mind and a body that are completely transparent. The field, the stars, the air, and the earth are all a part of our being. The awesome beauty, the power of the moment, the gentleness of the breeze, the hardness of the ground, and the chill of the settling dew all become a part of our existence. This is the power of mindfulness, to be completely present and transparent.

Having developed a sense of complete transparency, imagine sensing the existence of a power much greater than ourselves. The majesty of the vista that our transparent body participates in witnesses to a Creative Being that is part of and beyond the creation we participate in. Our very existence bears witness to this Being's loving nature, bringing forth life and nurture in the midst of this majestic openness.

In recognizing the existence of this Creative Being, we also recognize the Divine nature that is a part of who we are, giving us the power to think, and to love, and to reach beyond the confines of our human flesh that anchors us to the ground. We sense Divine Thought, Love, and Wisdom reaching out to us, embracing us, filling us with hope, love, and faith.

We sense our own Divine Nature glowing within us, like a beacon in the night, part of creation and in communion with the Creator who has chosen out of love to be a part of us. Filled to the point of overflowing, we sense the Divine attributes of hope, love, and faith emanating from us and touching others. Our Divine body glows with a Divine Light.

Finally, having recognized our nature as being transparent and Divine, we find ourselves recognizing other living creatures around us in this open field on this clear night. Our consciousness widens to recognize plants and animals in the field. Our consciousness widens even further to recognize people whom we love and people whom we dislike, those whom we know, and others whom we don't know. We recognize both the aspirations and the suffering that we hold in common with all living beings, the aspirations for freedom and happiness, and the suffering that comes when our aspirations are disappointed. Recognizing our common aspirations and common suffering draws out a sense of compassion for ourselves and for others. We recognize our own humanity.

Having recognized our transparent Spirit selves, our glowing Divine selves, and our living Human selves, we feel whole and at peace, and all the aspects of who we are draw together into one. We simply are - individuals connected with Others, Creation, and the Divine Creator.

In this open field, we are witnesses to the open transparency, the living Divinity, and the aspirations and suffering that all humans, indeed all of creation, hold in common. We feel both humbled and joyful. We breathe deeply and with a sense of gratitude.

Christian Tantric Meditation is a practice that moves through a definitive process.

Christian Tantric Meditation describes a collection of practices that provide a path for individuals to experience growth and liberation in recognizing and embracing the true nature of who we are, made in the image of God.

Christian Tantric Meditation is a process that includes developing mindfulness, communion with Divinity through Christ, and extending compassion towards self and others.

Christian Tantric meditation is an exercise for the mind, heart, and core areas of consciousness. By exercising these areas of consciousness, a person increases her or his capacity for mindfulness, love, self confidence, and compassion.

KEY CONCEPTS

In order to engage in Christian Tantric Meditation, we need to develop an understanding of the language and concepts used during meditation. The language of Christian Tantric Meditation is taken from both the Christian and Buddhist cultures.   It may be surprising how many concepts illustrated in tantric meditation language also apply to Judeo-Christian culture and scriptures. These concepts are common to many cultures, even beyond Christianity and Buddhism.

For example, the concepts of consciousness, love, and spirit are associated with being human in many cultures, and models have been developed to understand what it means to be human in those terms. In this chapter, we will describe a model for these concepts that allows us to explore and develop insight into our nature as human beings throughout the meditation practice.

The understanding of humanity existing in relationship with Divinity is also common to many cultures. Although western theologians often express the relationship of God with humans as being separated, the eastern ideas of Divinity and Humanity existing in close communion and sharing common characteristics are present in Judeo-Christian scripture. Humanity, after all, was created in the image of God. In this chapter, we will further explore our nature as human beings in relationship with Divinity.

We will also describe terminology that is integral to the practice of meditation.   The terms mindfulness, equanimity, and nonduality help us to understand how our consciousness evolves as we practice meditation.

These terms are like seeds that develop deeper and broader meaning as we move forward in the Christian Tantric Meditation practice.

Chakras and Flows – A Metaphysical Model

We are all familiar with physical models. In physics, substances are modeled in terms of energy, atoms, molecules, compounds, and so on. Similarly, in biology, living creatures are modeled in terms of sub-cellular elements, cells, organs, and increasingly complex organisms.

Prior to these modern physical models, other models existed. Substances were modeled in terms of earth, wind, fire, and water. Biological models included similar elements like humours (fluids), Breath/Spirit, Substance (earth), and even fire as a source of internal heat. In both traditional and modern models, materials and energy are understood to be ingredients in both organic and inorganic substances.

As the traditional models were replaced by newer models that explained and predicted more complex interactions and behaviors between the various elements, the prior models were not abandoned. They were given the term "metaphysical," and generally thought of in more mystical terms. The elements used within the models were assigned meaning beyond their physical attributes.

Metaphysical models are especially prevalent when thinking in terms of both humanity and Divinity, and in understanding relationships as well. Ideas like consciousness, sub-consciousness, faith and love, and even evil and hatred, are generally understood as being real but not easily modeled in a physical sense.

Both Eastern and Western metaphysical models have tended to focus more heavily on invisible forces that describe and direct human existence and behavior rather than physical substance, but physical substance is still a part of the discussion. For example, in Western Christian culture, Aristotle's writings regarding "substance" of living things are still the basis for understanding the mystery of the Divine Trinity. The concepts of Breath/Spirit, Consciousness/God, and Logos/Christ, form the foundation of the Christian Trinitarian metaphysical model. Christian Creeds have been written expressing the "Substance of God" as the basis for God's existence as a single Triune Being.

In the Eastern tantric metaphysical model of human substance, two concepts are used: chakras or energy centers, and channels through which energy flows. Chakras are considered physical centers of metaphysical attributes, such as consciousness, love, and wisdom, to name a few. In addition to chakras, channels are described that connect the chakras and facilitate the flow of breath energies through the entire body. Through these channels, the attributes of the chakras flow and co-mingle. This flow is described in terms of breath or breezes that flow throughout the body and can even flow beyond the confines of the body. This flow is the energy of life. Where there is life, life's energy flows. When life stops, breath energy stops flowing through the channels and leaves the body.

For the purpose of Christian Tantric Meditation, three main chakras are considered. These chakras are located in three corresponding areas of the body: the Mind which is the seat of hope and conscious awareness, the Heart which is the seat of love and compassion, and the Core, which is the seat of wisdom and faith. The core chakra is located just below the navel and a few inches in front of the spine, buried in one's viscera. For women practitioners, one might imagine the core chakra as the location of the womb, which is the source of creative life.

In the Chinese medicinal model, Breath/Spirit energy is known as chi. It is thought that blockages to chi within the body result in illness.

9

This is the core concept behind many eastern healing practices, including acupuncture, massage, and Rei Ki (Ki is the Japanese word for chi.) Allowing the healthy flow of energy between chakras and throughout the body is also a key concept in tantric meditation.

Chi is used to describe life energy in terms of vapor or breath or breeze. The same is true for the Greek word Pneuma, and the Hebrew word Ruach, used in the original Christian and Jewish scripture texts. The connection of breath, breeze, and the energy of life is well established in many cultures. For a deeper understanding of the concept of chakras and flows, refer to "Introduction to Tantra: The Transformation of Desire" by Lama Yeshe (Yeshe, 2001).

Human and Divine Nature

In a metaphysical sense, eastern and western philosophers and theologians recognize human beings as being both physical and Divine in nature. Indeed, Christians are well versed in the idea that humans are made "in God's image." Christians recognize a congruence, or similarity, between the natures of humanity and Divinity. Christian doctrine holds that this congruence was demonstrated in the person of Jesus the Christ.

It is tempting to think of humanity and Divinity in dualistic terms, but Christian Trinitarian thought asks us to think in **nondual** terms that recognize both humanity and Divinity in the person of Christ. Not "either or", but both. Indeed, many Christian scriptures tell us that through knowing Christ, we can gain an understanding of our own nature as well. Not only is Christ both human and Divine, so are we. Hence the Christian metaphysical model for humanity includes souls that exist for an eternity, even after the organic flesh dies and decomposes.

As a religious culture, Christianity describes God in terms of three nondual coexistent manifestations of the One Being: the Father, the Son, and the Holy Spirit. Christians recognize the Father in terms of omniscient consciousness, Jesus the Son in terms God's Immanent physical expression of love in the universe, and the Spirit as the source of Life and the Immanent expression of God's presence in day to day living.

Christians also associate God's female aspect with Spirit. God's female aspect is also described in the book of Ecclesiastes as the Wisdom of Sophia; and many Christian's relate to God's female aspect through Jesus' Mother Mary, the Mother of God.

Traditional tantric meditation recognizes the role of sexuality in one's sense of wholeness and well being. Indeed, tantric practices have been developed that focus solely on sexuality. But sexuality is not the sole focus of true tantric meditation; sexuality is understood as an integral part of who human beings are.

From a Judeo-Christian perspective, the creation story describes a whole human adam being separated into male and female counterparts, Adam and Eve. The implication is that at one time, humans were whole beings, and the joining of male and female counterparts can recreate the experience of being whole.

Tantric practice emphasizes the idea that in order to be whole humans, we need to be in touch with and accepting of both the male and female aspects of who we are as people. For female practitioners, this may mean emphasizing and accepting the Conscious Awareness that has been traditionally viewed as a male attribute. For male practitioners, this may mean emphasizing and accepting the Wisdom and Faithfulness that are traditionally identified as female attributes.

With this in mind, we introduce the understanding that the mind chakra, center of conscious awareness, corresponds with the Divine

11

aspect of God as the Father, the heart chakra, center of love and compassion, corresponds with the Divine aspect of God as the Child Jesus, and the core chakra, center of wisdom and faith, corresponds with the Divine aspect of God as the Mother Mary-Sophia. The Breath Life Energy, which flows through and between these chakras and binds them in nondual relationship, corresponds with the Holy Spirit.

Mindfulness, Equanimity, and Nonduality

Another concept to be aware of while practicing tantric meditation is **mindfulness**. Mindfulness is all about being in the here and now, in the moment, fully experiencing every aspect of life through every sense available. Mindfulness is also about being self aware of who we are, and accepting ourselves, the people we encounter, and the environment we live in. By knowing and accepting who we are, the people we know, and our environment, we develop the means to grow beyond our limitations.

Through the practice of tantric meditation, self awareness naturally develops. We learn about the influences in our lives that make us frustrated, anxious, depressed, or even give us physical pain. Mindfulness gives us the ability to detach from our pain and anxiety in a healthy way and look at ourselves objectively. When faced with pain and anxiety, many people react in impulsive and unhealthy ways. By observing ourselves and our pain objectively, we can choose to act in ways that are healthy and promote healing.

Mindfulness is introduced in the initial "Grounding" stage of Christian Tantric Meditation, and is an integral part of every stage of Christian Tantric Meditation. Throughout the practice, we develop mindfulness of our environment and surroundings, our inner mind processes, our heart centered processes, and our core centered processes.

While mindfulness is about being aware of self, **equanimity** is about understanding the common thread that binds all of humanity, and indeed all of creation.

In Matthew 5:43-48, Jesus talks about loving enemies, and how loving enemies is part of God's nature. Jesus asks us to love our enemies so that we might be "perfect, even as God is perfect." In this commandment and others, we are reminded that everyone is loved by God, and in the context of God's infinite Love, all are loved equally.

When viewed from the perspective of the ocean, all water drops are embraced equally. In the context of the life giving presence of the sun, all plants, indeed all living creatures, receive radiant warmth equally. God makes the sun to shine on both the just and the unjust, because God loves everyone unconditionally.

Equanimity is also an integral part of every stage of Christian Tantric Meditation. Throughout the practice, we develop an understanding of our equanimity with all of humanity in our mind centered processes, our heart centered processes, and our core centered processes.

One final concept that has already been introduced is **nonduality**. While equanimity helps us understand that we have much in common with each other, nonduality reminds us that we are individuals and we are all connected. We are connected to others, we are connected to the environment, we are connected to our past and to our future, and we are connected within our own transparent, Divine, and human natures.

The process that began our existence as individuals started with the creation of the Universe. If we think in terms of the Big Bang, we recognize that the matter and the energy which comprise the substance of who we are as people has been present literally from the beginning of time. And the substance of who we are has also been developing, from energy to atoms, from atoms to compounds, from compounds to living organisms, and so on. We have been developing through our ancestral lines as well.

Christ revealed that He was with the Father at Creation; in a very real sense we were present at the time of Creation as well. In a material as well as a metaphysical sense, we have always existed and we always will. We are intimately connected to the Universe, to each other, and to our ancestors.

While it's true we are all connected, it's also true that we are all individuals. Nonduality recognizes that we are connected and we are individuals. We are both.

How often do we struggle with what are known as false dichotomies? Very often, a lot of pain can be avoided by answering questions that involve "either/or" with "yes." Yes, I am a parent and a child of my parents. Yes I am a working person and a family person. Yes, I am human and I am Divine in nature, even as Jesus the Christ was and is human and Divine. Yes, I am a product of my environment, my past, my ancestry, and my family and friends, and yes I am my own person. Recognizing this "yes" is the essence of nonduality, and a very important concept on the journey of accepting ourselves and others. And acceptance leads to healing and growth.

Nonduality is also an integral part of every stage of Christian Tantric Meditation. Throughout the practice, we are reminded of our connection with ourselves, the Divine, humanity, and creation.

To summarize, we've introduced the ideas of chakras and flows, and we've reinforced the idea that humanity was created in the image of God. We have also applied the use of chakras and flows to the Christian Trinitarian metaphysical model. Finally, we introduced the terms mindfulness, equanimity, and nonduality to help us understand our human nature and our relationship with Divinity.

INTRODUCTORY PRACTICE: GROUNDING AND MINDFULNESS

Having developed an understanding of some of the key concepts involved in Christian Tantric Meditation practice, we need to develop an understanding of the process and core skills that are used throughout the practice. Each stage of the practice builds on the skills developed in the previous stages.

In this chapter, we describe the pace at which to proceed while practicing meditation. We also explore the relative merits of pursuing the practice alone or with a partner, and the role that outside support can play while engaging in the practice. Finally, we will describe core skills that are used in every stage of the practice, including mindful breathing and space oriented projection.

Taking time through the process

As we begin the process of tantric meditation, we need to be mindful of the pace at which we progress. Everyone is different, so there is no set rate or pace. The process starts with warm-up practices and continues into the individual stages of practice from there.

We all know that people are different. Some people are naturally peaceful and patient, while others are high strung and energetic. Often, people who have high energy levels and maybe even anxiety seek out meditation as a means of slowing down and relaxing. Unfortunately, those same people often become impatient with the process of meditation and give up after a short time.

Tantric meditation can help with this because it provides a process to follow. A person has the opportunity to pace themselves. Meditation practitioners recommend becoming comfortable with one stage before moving through to the next. While that is recommended for this practice as well, it's generally OK to read ahead and try the different stages that follow. However it is recommended that a person develop an ability to dwell at any stage for at least 15 to 20 minutes. A useful tool for this might be a smartphone application that is used for meditation purposes. It is possible to configure a meditation application to signal "gongs" at regular intervals to help a person to pace themselves.

A beginner may practice the warm-up stage for a month before feeling comfortable with the exercises, but may read ahead and try subsequent stages as well. After a month of practice, a person may pass through the warm-up more quickly (a few minutes) and spend more time dwelling within a later stage that they are working on becoming comfortable with.

Eventually, as we become comfortable with the entire process, we find that the stage we dwell at varies from session to session. For example, an experienced practitioner who is working through a challenging week may just practice self emptying exercises and not even proceed to later stages. Or a person feeling a need for healing may move quickly into "Divine Communion" stage and dwell there for an extended period. The stage at which a person dwells varies even for experienced practitioners.

Having a guide or a partner in the process

Tantric Buddhist texts recommend that practice be undertaken with a

Guru or guide. While this is good advice, a Guru is not always readily available, and the fact is that people like to read through instructional books and begin practice on their own.

The risks of not having a Guru or a guide while practicing include giving up the practice due to lack of encouragement, lacking guidance when disturbing memories or feelings appear while practicing, and developing "bad habits" while practicing.

The encouragement issue can be mitigated by practicing with a partner, even a partner who is also inexperienced. As with physical exercise, having a partner can help motivate and encourage continued practice.

The issue of activating uncomfortable feelings while practicing can be helped by having a partner to talk to as well. Most people process uncomfortable feelings and memories by sharing with people they feel they can trust. Sharing is a natural healing process.

It's also OK to practice meditation without a partner. Like any exercise, if discomfort arises, a person has to adjust. Some people cross train physically to avoid repetitive stress injuries. For example, a person may alternate Yoga or Tai Chi with an activity such as biking or walking. When it comes to meditation, the tantric method is a natural cross training practice for the mind. Emptying and fulfillment are balanced, as are inward and outward consciousness foci. If an area of meditation brings emotional pain, a person has the option to take a break from the practice, adjust the practice, or get help in the form of friendship guidance or even professional counseling. Seeking help in conjunction with tantric meditation can be a powerfully liberating experience.

One of the benefits of Christian Tantric Meditation is that it incorporates practices from several disciplines, including mindfulness, compassion, and Guru Yoga practices. A person can limit the development of "bad habits" by engaging in meditation classes and retreats from almost any tradition. Whether oriented towards mindful stress reduction, Vipassana insight development, Lojang compassion training, or even Christian Tantric Meditation itself, the skills learned while taking classes will validate and enhance the CTM experience.

Practicing CTM independently would be similar to a person practicing Yoga or Tai Chi with an instructional DVD, and later taking a class with an instructor. Once in the class, the practitioner may find that she or he has been using imperfect postures or breathing, but these behaviors can be corrected. In the mean time, strength has been developed while using the DVD that other students may not have, even if every posture is not performed perfectly.

One other note to make about practicing CTM with or without a class or partner. In CTM, the recognition of an unconditionally loving Deity is part of the process. This means Deity in the Trinitarian sense, with God the Father representing Divine Consciousness, Jesus the Christ representing unconditional love and compassion, and Mary Sophia representing wisdom and faith. The Holy Spirit is also present as the breath energy that is shared within the Trinity with the practitioner, and is extended towards others in compassion as part of the practice.

Given that Divine presence is part of the practice, a person is never truly alone when practicing CTM. This thought and understanding can bring comfort and healing to the practitioner.

Mindful Breathing.

For many who meditate, mindful breathing is the only practice that is needed. Indeed, for some who read this guide, the practice of mindful breathing may be sufficient and the rest of the tantric practice may serve for informational purposes only.

A wonderful text to read as we practice mindful breathing is "The Miracle of Mindfulness" by Thich Nhat Hanh. (Hanh, 1975) The discussions and techniques discussed in Hahn's book can serve as a solid foundation for developing mindful living and practice.

Posture is important during meditation. A comfortable upright position is preferred. This could be in a chair, or on a cushion on the floor with one's seat elevated above the knees. A straight posture facilitates deep breathing and comfort over an extended period.

The process of mindful breathing is very natural. It starts with inhaling slowly through the nose, and then exhaling slowly through the nose or mouth.

As we inhale, we notice how it feels to have our lungs expand. We notice how it feels to have air pass through our nose and into our lungs. We notice how it feels to release the pressure from our lungs as we exhale. We feel our chest rising and falling. We move towards expanding our core as we breathe, and we notice how expanding our stomach area deepens our breathing experience.

As we breathe, we naturally relax. Thoughts naturally wander through our mind. We accept our thoughts, and let them go with each exhale, bringing our attention back to our breathing. This is called centering.

While practicing centering, we may experience itching in areas of our body. It's OK to scratch if we need to scratch. Above all we are kind to ourselves as we breathe. We accept the itches, and let them go. We accept the thoughts, and let them go. We return to our center, our breathing.

Various visualizations have been suggested for allowing thoughts and feelings to pass. We may visualize thoughts floating away on a breeze, like clouds against a blue sky. We may visualize ourselves next to a river or creek, and allow our thoughts and feelings to float away. As our thoughts drift away, our attention always returns to our breathing.

We may develop a core word that brings us back to center. This is what Richard Foster suggests in his book called "Prayer." (Foster, 1992) He recognizes meditation as a sort of "listening prayer." And listening is what we are doing, in being aware of ourselves, accepting our thoughts and feelings, and letting them float away. Our core word may be "peace," or "love," or even a short verse from scripture. As thoughts pass through, we wrap them in our word and let them float away.

At first, sitting for 5 minutes and breathing may be very difficult. That's OK. It takes time to develop this skill. Accepting the challenge, we breathe for as long as we are comfortable. Over time, we find that we become comfortable breathing for as long as 20 to 30 minutes.

Breathing in and of itself is a very relaxing thing to do. By practicing relaxed breathing for at least 5 minutes per day, we program our bodies to relax when we breathe intentionally. When we are out living our lives, we may find ourselves in tense or anxious situations. When these situations arise, we may eventually find that one intentional breath helps wash away the anxiety as a conditioned response to the practice of mindful breathing.

We may visualize the Holy Spirit participating in our breathing, offering us cleansing healing breezes with every inhale. We may visualize negative influences like pain and anxiety leaving our bodies with every exhale.

In preparation for tantric practice, we may visualize our chakras and connecting flow channels as we breathe. We may visualize our inward breath flowing through our channels, connecting and cleansing our chakras. If we have areas of physical discomfort in our bodies, we may visualize the energy flow caressing and soothing the areas that may be blocking our natural pathways. Even emotional discomfort can often be associated with areas of our body. If we feel anxiety in our core, we may visualize our breath flowing around and through our core, bringing soothing comfort and healing.

This process of developing one's ability to breath in a mindful manner will take time. How long the development takes depends on the individual. It may take a few days, it may take a few weeks. Some people choose to practice mindful breathing for several months before moving on to the next stage.

Space Oriented Projection:

Another warm up practice that is helpful is known as projection. The practice of projection has been used for as long as humanity has had imagination. In the legend of King Arthur, young Arthur was asked by Merlin to imagine that he could see through the eyes of a flying bird. As the legend goes, this "projection practice" led to formation of the Round Table counsel.

Traditions such as Astral Projection, Tantric Phowa in preparation for death, Guru Yoga practices, and "The Six Yogas of Naropa" (Mullin,1996) all reference projection practices. Even in the Christian bible, Jesus commands us to "love your neighbor as yourself" (Matt 22:39), which asks us to imagine what it would be like to walk in the shoes of another.

The interplay of objects and the space they occupy in relation to meditative exercises are discussed in Tarthang Tulku's book "Time, Space, and Knowledge." (Tulku, 1977) In his book Tulku describes the "relaxation and satisfaction benefits" associated with altering one's "focal setting" to recognize space rather than objects. (Tulku, 1977, location 343 Kindle Edition)

In 1976, prior to the release of his book, Tulku provided a retreat and seminar at his Nyingma Institute in Berkley, Ca. with renowned biofeedback researcher Joe Kamiya. The seminar emphasized "The interface between the Nyingma Tradition of Tibetan Buddhism and the seeds of developing Western Psychology." (Advertisement, 1976)

Biofeedback research into these meditative practices revealed that "space oriented projection" exercises can lead the brain into a relaxed state. When the brain is led into this state, one can observe calm, synchronous brain activity using EEG equipment. Under normal circumstances, the brain registers a chaotic variety of activity. Meditative techniques can lead the brain into a relaxed state without the aid of external equipment. These findings were documented and applied to the control of pain in the books "Open Focus Brain" by Les Fehmi and Jim Robbins (Fehmi, 2007), and "Dissolving Pain". (Fehmi, 2010)

The basic space oriented projection exercise involves imagining the space an object occupies, rather than focusing on an object directly. This remarkable practice serves the purpose of taking one's consciousness to the object, rather than bringing the object into one's mind.

For example, if there is a chair in the room, and we close our eyes and imagine the chair, we bring the image of the chair into our minds. However, if we imagine the space that the chair occupies, we carry our consciousness to the chair. We effectively project our consciousness to the space where the chair resides.

For the purpose of meditation, we begin by taking several deep cleansing breaths, as we have practiced already, and centering ourselves. Then we imagine the space occupied by areas within our bodies. We imagine the space occupied by our left foot. As we imagine that space, we allow our consciousness to dwell there for several seconds. We imagine the space occupied by our right elbow. Our jaw. Our left thigh. We allow our consciousness to dwell within each of these spaces for some period of time.

As we move our consciousness around our bodies, we become very relaxed. We find we are breathing in a relaxed manner without even thinking about it.

For the purpose of tantric practice, we move our consciousness through the spaces that our chakras occupy. In doing so, we move into the first stage of Christian Tantric Practice: self emptying.

Projecting our consciousness to our energy centers naturally increases our mindfulness. When our consciousness dwells within our mind, we become aware of the thoughts that naturally arise and we normally don't notice. When our consciousness dwells within our heart, we become aware of both the love and resentments we hold towards ourselves and others. And when our consciousness dwells within our core centers, we become aware of the inner strength and fears. Our overall self awareness can increase dramatically with this practice.

Having developed an understanding of pacing and utilizing outside resources, and having developed a basic understanding of mindful breathing and space oriented projection, we are ready to move forward to the first stage in Christian Tantric Meditation Practice: Self Emptying.

STAGE ONE: SELF EMPTYING

The practice of self emptying is an essential beginning to any form of tantric practice. Self emptying is described in great detail in Lama Yeshe's book "Introduction to Tantra" (Yeshe, 2001).

Self emptying is a process of letting go of the desires, resentments, and fears that clutter our lives. When we empty ourselves of these distractions, we become free to realize our potential as human beings. We become free to observe and be a part of all that is.

Before engaging in self emptying, we need to develop a clear understanding of our motivations for engaging in meditative practice. As we begin to release our desires, resentments, and fears, we may develop a sense of emptiness. We need to remember the positive goals that brought us to the practice in the first place. We also need to be kind to ourselves, and be willing to engage outside resources such as journaling, talking about our experiences and feelings with friends, and possibly even professional therapy if needed.

The practice of self emptying is not intended to leave a vacuum within us. The practice is intended to reduce our internal distractions so that we may experience life to its fullest. The awareness we develop during our self emptying exercise expands and draws us outside of ourselves, allowing our attention to expand beyond the bounds that pull us inward and hold us back.

Self emptying happens in three stages. At first we dwell within our mind chakra, letting go of desires that distract, hurt, and hold us back. We also cultivate awareness of the hope, freedom, and opportunity that are present in our lives as we let go of our self limiting desires.

Next we dwell within our heart chakra, letting go of our resentments. We also begin cultivating awareness of the unconditional love that is available and surrounds and fills us as we let go of the resentments that isolate us.

And finally, we dwell within our core chakra, releasing the fears that hold us back. We also develop an awareness of the faithfulness and strength that surrounds and lifts us when we let go of the fears that hold us back.

As we dwell in each of these areas, the desires, resentments, and fears we hold probably won't dissolve completely. When we emerge from our meditation, our rent or mortgage payments, car payments, our relatives with ailments, and our own ailments may still be present. But if we can release our burdens for the 20 minutes we are engaged in meditation, we get a vacation from them and we loosen the grip they have on our lives. We become better equipped to deal with our ongoing challenges, and we develop the ability to fully experience life without the distractions of those burdens.

Step One: Releasing Desires from the Mind

From a Christian perspective, desires are often associated with sin. Because the word "sin" generally promotes isolation and shame rather than healing, it can be more helpful to use the word "harm" instead.

Harmful desires interfere with us reaching our full potential. Harmful desires can bring suffering to ourselves and the people who love us. They can steal our lives and livelihoods. Harmful desires may include addictions, the desire to control others, and even the desire to harm ourselves or others.

Even the desires that we don't interpret as "harmful", including the desires for success and happiness, can interfere with achieving success and happiness.

Remember the parable from Christian Scripture of the landowner who built the second barn to hold his grain harvest (Luke 12:13-21). The time and effort he put into building the barn took away from his life and joy. He thought he was going to be happier, but in the end his desire for security just took away from his life. He sacrificed the "here and now" for the illusion of future happiness.

Happiness is here and now. Success may come from hard work and dedication, but the desire to possess can distract from a person's ability to do the things necessary to achieve success. We can hardly do our jobs if we are preoccupied with vacation houses or boats or even the security of our families. To be truly successful we need to lay our desires down in order to be fully present in our lives. Indeed, individuals who allow their desires to interfere with their occupational tasks are sometimes tempted to use unethical conduct in order to achieve those desires. When we can release our desires and fully immerse ourselves – mindfully – into whatever task we undertake, success will come.

Opportunities can also be lost due to desires. There is another story regarding a person who is on a roof in the midst of a flood. Rescue boats and helicopters come to the aid of the person, but the person refuses help, insisting that Jesus will intervene on his behalf. Eventually, the person drowns, and later in heaven the person asks Jesus why He did not intervene. In the story Jesus responds that He had sent boats and helicopters, but those opportunities for rescue were refused. This person may have harbored a desire to be lifted like the prophet Elijah from the roof. His desire blinded him to alternative opportunities that presented themselves. While this story illustrates a rescue, the same can hold true for career or employment opportunities, for relationship opportunities, and for opportunities to simply enjoy life.

Have you ever met a person who is truly driven? For example, someone who is driven to please the Lord? People who are so focused on reading scripture and attending worship sometimes miss simple opportunities to be friendly with others and be present for their families. Even in the context of "Pleasing the Lord," being fully present is the most we can do. Pleasing the Lord requires recognizing the Lord in our day to day lives, in the people we meet and in the tasks that we perform. And recognizing the Lord requires us to be fully present and mindful. It's hard to be mindful when our minds are cluttered with distractions and desires, harmful and not.

Western society tends to emphasize being goal driven (future oriented) as a way to achieve success. In a sense, our consciousness exists in a continuum that extends from the past, through the present, and into the future. Some people dwell on past glories and hope for restoration. Others dwell on future goals and hope for success. The motivation behind mindfulness meditation and releasing desires is to bring one's consciousness into the here and now, into the present. In the here and now, freedom and opportunities are available.

Biographies of successful people often reveal an ability to recognize and capitalize on opportunities as they arise. In contrast, people who are obsessively future or goal oriented may miss opportunities due to their lack of attention to the here and now. Sometimes we feel shackled by our goals as life literally passes us by while we work for a future that we hold in our imaginations.

That's not to say that having goals is a bad thing. It is reasonable to have goals in mind while living in the present moment. Goals can help us set a general direction for our lives to follow as long as they don't exclude present moment opportunities.

Alternatively, sometimes we may feel shackled by our past as we hold on to old relationships, losses, and even traumatic experiences. There is great value in being aware of our past. It is possible to be aware of the events and relationships that helped to shape us while living in the present moment.

With this in mind, the first step of Christian Tantric Meditation is directing one's attention towards the mind chakra. We imagine the space that our mind occupies. We rest our consciousness in that space for a few breaths. We rest our consciousness in that space for a few minutes. This is the space where all our thoughts originate, the thoughts that lead to our actions. This is the space where we sense physical pain; pain that originates in areas of our bodies is processed within our minds. This is the space where we translate our feelings into words, we interpret things we read and we recognize people and places we experience. The mind is the center of how we conduct our day to day activities.

As we imagine the space that our mind occupies, our desires may appear to us as thoughts. At first our harmful urges and material desires may arise. Using mindful breathing, with every exhale we let them drift away like clouds in the sky. In Christian language, this conscious act of acknowledging and releasing our harmful desires is confession.

After releasing harmful desires, desires that we view as reasonable and wholesome may appear. These desires may include goals, like getting a better job or a better education, or improving ourselves or our relationships. By releasing the desirous aspect of our goals, we free ourselves to enjoy the tasks we perform rather than being enslaved to them. These desires also drift away on the clouds.

We may also view desires related to attachments that we hold on to from the past. Our desire for restoration to a sense of wholeness may drift across the clear sky of our consciousness. With a sense of great kindness towards ourselves, we let our attachments to the past, both positive and negative, drift away as well, leaving us in the here and now with a sense of peace and hopefulness.

The process of surrendering desires may involve imagining letting them float away on a breeze, or drift away in a stream. We may visualize tossing them in an ocean and watching them float away on the tide. Or, as Christians, we may lay our desires down at the foot of the Cross, and offer them up to God in an act of sacrifice. As we watch our desires dissolve at the foot of the Cross, our gaze moves upward and again we witness a clear blue sky consciousness.

This first step of releasing our desires can take a long time to accomplish. We may find ourselves thinking about letting go of our desires even when we do not meditate. This is a natural part of the process. The work we do in meditation stays with us in our day to day lives.

As we renounce our desires, we may also engage in a process of mourning. If we want to be totally honest, our desires actually bring great comfort to us. They offer escape, they offer solace, they provide a "me only" shelter for our selfish needs. As we let these go, we may find ourselves a little lost.

As we go through this process over time, we need to constantly remind ourselves to be kind and understanding with ourselves. Thich Nhat Hanh wrote a book called "Embracing the Inner Child" (Hahn, 2010). In the book Hanh advises that we learn to recognize our inner child when negative feelings emerge. We need to offer ourselves solace. We need to embrace our inner child who feels unfulfilled and perhaps would rather throw a tantrum than allow us to release our desires. We can allow our adult selves to hug and reassure our inner child.

When we release our desires, we become joyfully free to experience life, and the people and places and things we encounter. We free ourselves to become a part of our reality, here and now. We become free to accept opportunities that exist here and now. We become free to live, free to love, and free to be. Having experienced these revelations of freedom and joy, when ready, we return to our centered breathing. Breathing in and out, we are at peace.

When are we ready to move on to the next step, the heart chakra? At first we may dwell within our mind chakra for only a few minutes, but we need to master this step before we can move on in earnest. We can move forward and experiment with later steps, but until we are comfortable with achieving an open mind, we need to concentrate our efforts here. While releasing desires may make sense to us intellectually, we need to achieve a deeper understanding. We need to feel it. It needs to become a part of us. And that takes time. We need to be able to dwell comfortably for several minutes in our mind chakra with a clear blue sky consciousness before we can say we are truly ready to dwell within later steps.

Step Two: Releasing Resentments and Attachments from the Heart

After developing the practice of resting our consciousness within the space that our mind occupies, we move our consciousness to the space that our heart occupies. The heart is the center of love. The heart reaches out to others, and the heart receives love from others. The chi energy that our heart generates flows through our other chakras and emanates outward toward others. Imagine the space our heart occupies. We rest our consciousness in our heart for a few breaths. We rest our consciousness in our heart for a few minutes.

Unfortunately, our hearts are not only filled with love. They are often filled with resentment and pain, and scars from hurtful encounters. With a little effort we can surrender those resentments and pains. We can use the same techniques we used when surrendering our desires. We can let our resentments drift away on the wind or in a stream. We can cast them into the ocean and they float away on the current. Or, as Christians, we can offer them up to God at the foot of the Cross.

We might imagine our hearts as bowls that are filled with old hurts and resentments. As we hold on to those resentments, there is no space for Divine Love to enter our hearts and flow through us and beyond us. Only by opening our hearts can we hope to have our hearts filled with healing Grace.

Along with hurts and resentments, unhealthy attachments may also reside within our hearts. Being human, it can be easy to confuse love with attachment. The heart is the center of love, and love cannot flourish if it is bound by attachment.

In Lorne Ladner's book entitled "The Lost Art of Compassion" (Ladner 2004), she discusses the difference between attachment and love in terms of desiring to be close to someone versus wishing for their happiness and well being. Most loving relationships include both love and attachment, but a healthy question to ask is whether our desire to be close to someone is stronger than our hope for their happiness and well being. Heart centered self emptying offers an opportunity to release attachments so that only love remains in the heart.

Attachment also causes us to impose unhealthy expectations on others. Love can be expressed in many ways. If we expect love to come to us in a particular form or manner, we miss out on love expressed in ways we can't even imagine.

As we dwell within our heart centers and release our hurts, resentments, and unhealthy attachments, our inner child may surface. We may discover that we need those resentments, hurts, and attachments. We may have held on to them for so long that they are like old friends now. Like our harmful desires, they may actually bring us a sense of comfort.

We can be kind to ourselves as we let them go. We can visualize our adult self hugging our inner child, reassuring ourselves that all is well. We can trust that the space we create within our hearts can be filled with Divine Love.

At first we may dwell for only a few minutes within the space our heart occupies, and we may decide to try further steps. This is OK. We may experience emotional discomfort and choose to return to our centered breathing, relaxed and cleansing. We may struggle with this for a fairly long time, months even. That's OK also. There is always time for love and healing. It takes time to build up resentments, it takes time to let them go.

We may want to write in a journal, or talk about our experiences with others. This can help us to let go and move on.

We may even reach a place where we are comfortable while we meditate, but we notice our old resentments return in our day to day lives. This is fine, in fact this is great, because as we take a vacation from our resentments, we loosen their grip on us. If we can take a vacation from our hurts and resentments while we meditate, we find that we can eventually let them go when we are engaged in our day to day living. We can love more deeply, we can work more effectively, we can experience more completely. We are taking another step in the direction toward liberation, mindfulness, and compassion.

As we relax and release our resentments, we also discover

resentments that are directed against ourselves. We may have hurt ourselves in addition to others during our lives. We may have held ourselves back from loving unconditionally, or we may have pushed ourselves too hard. Whatever the case, we can view ourselves with compassion and give ourselves a break, even if others are not willing to do so. The resentments, hurts, and attachments that hang on to us are real, but they are also manufactured by our circumstances and our past. We can give ourselves a break and let them go.

Our resentments, hurts, and attachments may be a part of us, but they do not define us. We are more than our desires, and we are more than our painful experiences. We are loved. We can find comfort in knowing and accepting this. And we can let our resentments, hurts, and attachments go.

As we let go of the resentments that hold us back, we begin to recognize the love that is all around us. There may be people in our lives who have tried to love us, but the hurts and resentments we hold in our hearts were too distracting or overpowering to allow us to recognize it.

As we let go of attachments, we begin to recognize love offered in ways we previously could not comprehend. People in our lives may have tried to love us, but our unhealthy expectations limited our ability to perceive and accept love.

We may start noticing the presence of trees and flowers and grasses and wildlife that we had been taking for granted. The smell of leaves in autumn, or the brightness of stars on a cold winter night, or the chirping of birds may remind us of a Divine love that has been present for us, calling to us, for a long, long time.

As we release our resentments with every exhale, and recognize pervasive love with every inhale, we can return to our centered breathing. In and out, relaxed and peaceful, we feel loved and whole.

Step 3: Releasing Fears and Burdens from our Core

After we are comfortable resting in our heart chakra, we move our consciousness to our core chakra. Imagine the space our core occupies. We breathe in and out, our energy circulates, and we rest there. Our core chakra is where our wisdom and faith resides. Our core chakra is our anchor, our center of gravity. We rest our consciousness there for several breaths, leading to several minutes.

As we rest our consciousness in our core, we let go of our fears and burdens that reside there. We surrender our fears and burdens to our Higher Power. We feel ourselves lighten as we let them go, one by one.

We let go of things we have control of and things we don't have control of, including the future, the past, financial issues, and family issues. We also begin to let go of people from our past or present whom we fear. We might even begin to let go of phobic obsessions like spiders or heights or closed spaces.

Hopefully by now we have established a visualization that works for us. Like our desires and our resentments before, we surrender our fears and burdens in the manner that is most comfortable for us. We may let them go with every exhale, letting them float away on a breeze. We may let them drift out on an ocean or down a stream. As Christians we may consciously lay them at the foot of the Cross. However we release our fears and burdens, we do so with a sense of kindness towards ourselves.

Of course, our burdens may not actually disappear, at least not at first. This is not magic. Bills still need to be paid, and we still have our families and our jobs and our lives. What we are doing is taking a little vacation from our burdens. We let them go and we experience a brief respite from them. Later on, as we deal with our burdens on a day to day basis, we may find them less burdensome. We find we can deal with them one at a time, so we do not feel overwhelmed.

The same is true of our fears. The deeper seated our fears are, the more time and patience it takes to release them fully. But every time we practice this meditation, we work on unraveling the knot that has been present in our cores for so long. The knot that holds us back, the knot that sits like a nagging ache in our gut, alternately bringing anxiety and depression to our lives gradually begins to loosen. And as the knot loosens, we may find that our fears eventually dissipate over time.

At first, we dwell within our core only for as long as we are comfortably able. Our fears and burdens are released and our sense of self esteem and security grows. This may only be for just a minute or two, but as we become more comfortable we may dwell here up to several minutes or longer.

As we release our fears and burdens, we begin to sense the support and strength and resiliency that surrounds us and is within us. We may recognize that even though we have felt alone, we are not alone. Realizing that others experience the same fears and burdens that we do helps us to feel less alone. We recognize that others are supportive and hopeful on our behalf, even when we have felt alone and hopeless. We begin to recognize the inner strengths that we are gifted with – and that builds our self esteem and confidence.

For some of us, the release of fears, resentments, and desires may be frightening. We may feel like we are losing our sense of self. Having defined ourselves for so long by our desires, our resentments and attachments, and our fears and burdens, we may not remember who we were without them. If anxiety arises, we return our attention to our centered breathing. This is our anchor through this entire process. We hear our breath, we feel our breath, we experience our breath. We relax.

We may discover that all these burdens and fears have kept our inner child hidden for many years. It's no wonder the only chance we have to touch our inner child is when she or he breaks through our consciousness and acts out with fear or anger. Once liberated from our fears, our inner child has the opportunity to once again experience the wonders of creation as if for the first time. Sand at the beach, grass on the ground, the color and texture of leaves, the intricacies of a grasshopper, they all become new to us again. Our curiosity emerges, and we begin to experience things more fully. Even a cup of coffee or tea or juice in the morning becomes a moment of celebration, experienced fully for its smell, its taste, and its texture.

We may also experience a sense of loss. We may mourn the passing of our desires, resentments, and fears. After all, they have been our companions for a long time. Remember the most important rule as we proceed through these exercises: be kind to ourselves. Its OK to cry if we need to. We can write in our journals, we can talk with a friend or an understanding pastor, or a counselor. And eventually, just like with any loss, we may find that we can accept and move on.

Extra Credit: Releasing Physical or Emotional Pain

The book "Dissolving Pain" by Les Fehmi (Fehmi, 2007) was mentioned previously as a good resource to utilize for developing the ability to direct our consciousness towards our chakras. It is also a wonderful guide for releasing physical and emotional pain. Releasing physical and emotional pain can be a part of the Christian Tantric Meditation process as well.

We have learned how to imagine the space where our chakras reside and empty ourselves of some of the forces that distract and control us. If we have a physical pain in an elbow, a sinus condition behind our eyes, or a strained back, we can use a similar process to dissipate the pain we experience in those and other areas. If we feel a knot of anxiety in our stomach, or a hollow emptiness of depression in our chest, we can also use these techniques to dissipate our emotional pain.

For example, if we have pain in an elbow, we can imagine the space where our elbow resides. Breathing deeply, we remember that our spirit, our life energy, our chi, flows beyond our chakras to every part of our bodies. When blockage occurs, chi has trouble flowing. As we rest our awareness in the space where our elbow resides, we consciously let go of the pain that is present there. With every inhale, Divine Energy floods to the area of pain, and with every exhale, the pain dissipates. We dwell here for several seconds. We visualize the space between our elbow and our shoulder. Our Spirit energy flows freely up to the point of our pain. We visualize the space between our elbow and our hand. Spirit flows freely around the area of pain and through our hand as well. As we expand our awareness to areas outside of our pain, we may sense that our pain dissipates. With every breath, our chi carries away the pain and with every exhale, and the pain dissipates.

The same exercise can be used for emotional pain. Emotional pain can often be associated with particular areas in our bodies, and for each individual, the area of pain may be different. Emotional pain may manifest as a tightness or emptiness in some part of the body, or it may manifest as actual physical pain. For example, emotional pain may manifest in the lower back or as a stiff neck. As we develop mindfulness, we become aware of ourselves and how we react to stresses and emotional pain.

The process for releasing emotional pain is the same. We imagine the space where our pain arises. That knot in our stomach, that hollow feeling in our chest, we imagine that space. We breathe deeply and allow our chi to flow in and around our areas of pain. We imagine the space between our pain and other areas of our body. Our chi flows freely through these areas and caresses our area of pain. Slowly, patiently, we allow our consciousness to move around and through our areas of pain. Slowly, patiently, we allow our chi energy to dissipate our pain.

Relief from pain is not instant, and for some it may not occur at all. Underlying causes to pain may remain, even if our pain is dissipated. Meditative healing is not a substitute for utilizing outside resources such as doctors and counselors. It is part of a holistic process of gaining self awareness, mindfulness, and allowing ourselves to accept healing from the many resources that are available for healing and wholeness.

Release Closing: Realizing our Transparent Self

Remember that tantric practice is in harmony with our Christian culture's understanding of God's Trinitarian nature. And remember that as Beings created in God's Image, we too carry this Trinitarian nature. This is why we proceed through the three chakras. While dwelling within our mind chakra and releasing our desires, we liberate our Divine Consciousness, which is created in the image of God the Father. While dwelling in our heart chakra and releasing our resentments, we open our Divine Loving-kindness, which is created in the image of God as Jesus the Christ, unconditionally loving and near at hand. As we dwell in our Core chakra and release our fears and burdens, we liberate our Divine Wisdom and Faithfulness, which is created in the image of God as Mother, Mary Sophia.

As we practice releasing our burdens in each of these chakra centers, we utilize our breath —our spirit energy, our chi, created in the image of the Holy Spirit, in sweeping through our chakras and cleaning out our desires, resentments, and fears. Our chi becomes light and free, and it moves easily within us, releasing the worries and pain that resides in our chakras and throughout our bodies.

As we complete the process of releasing the burdens that hold us back, we allow another version of ourselves, a transparent body, to arise. We imagine the space that our entire body occupies.

As we dwell in our newly risen transparent bodies, we experience mindfulness. Our inner child experiences the world as if it were a new place. We feel the air around us, filling our lungs and releasing. We sense the presence of others, near and far. We sense our nondual nature, shared with the ground underneath us, and the nature that surrounds us.

We are connected, and yet we are free. We are transparent. The world moves around and through us, we are a part of the Universe. We begin to realize what Jesus meant in saying "I am in the Father, and you are in me, and I am in you." (John 14:20) We begin to realize our Divine nature.

Resting in this space of transparency, we may begin to feel a sensation of Bliss. Lighter than air, we are truly free! We are free to experience the mindfulness, unconditional love, and freedom that we were created for! We prepared ourselves for the next stage in the process – Divine Communion.

As we release ourselves from this stage of meditation, we smile at ourselves. We smile at our inner child. We breathe deeply, and slowly emerge, feeling grounded and at peace. We take cleansing breaths as we slowly shake out our limbs.

Between our meditative sessions, we may find that our daily lives are not quite the same. We may find we begin to experience life more fully.

If we have children in our lives, we may allow our inner child to play with them and enjoy them more fully. If we have family and friends and intimate partners in our lives, we may relax a little and enjoy their company more fully. If we normally turn to alcohol or other means to relax in social situations, we may find we can begin to let that burden go, as the reasons for needing artificial relaxation or stimulation gradually and gently disappear. We may consume less in social situations, and eventually we may choose to consume nothing at all.

If we tend to self isolate, we may begin to seek out friends for our inner child to play with, to share with. If we tend to be very active socially, we may intentionally take time to commune with out inner sense of peace. This is natural, this represents a restoration of balance.

Reflection on Self Emptying – Identity

For many people, desires, resentments, and fears provide a lifetime of motivation. People formulate desires for careers, for relationships, and for circumstances of living. Others occupy their time reacting to resentments, either avoiding sources of pain or working towards unhealthy goals like revenge. Still others spend entire lifetimes striving for control in an attempt to manage their fears.

After some practice at self emptying meditation, desires, resentments, and fears eventually start to fade. As these motivations fade, a person may sense a vacuum or emptiness developing. An identity crisis of sorts can occur, which can lead to a "relapse" into the thinking and behaviors that the person strives to release through meditation.

Throughout the process of self emptying, we remind ourselves of the reasons we feel called to accept faith, love, and hopefulness. The point of self emptying is to open ourselves up so we can recognize and accept these gifts that are freely available.

The next stage of the practice, which may be called "Divine

Communion" or "Spiritual Awakening," can help alleviate our sense of loss. As we reach for Communion with the Divine, we begin to glimpse the Divine Being we were created to be. We start to glimpse our infinite potential that is not constrained by time or physical limitations. And we start to live our lives in ways that reflect this inner vision of our Divine Selves, in Communion with Divine God.

In the process we begin to replace "what we want" with "who we are." This is who we were created to be.

STAGE TWO: DIVINE COMMUNION

It may take several weeks or even months to fully assimilate the first stage of releasing ours desires, resentments, and fears. Even if we choose to move forward to experience further stages, we need to dwell at prior stages until they become a part of us. Like muscle memory developed after many hours of physical training, consciousness memory is developed as we dwell in each stage of meditation, until each experience becomes a part of us.

Buddhist practitioners describe being free from desires and attachments as a source of joy or bliss. Indeed, the release of burdens can be incredibly liberating and uplifting, and can be a source of joy. Modern tantric interpretations also associate joy with the liberation and sharing of inner sexual energy with an intimate partner.

When Christians speak of joy we often think of reconciliation or reunion. When the angels announced the birth of Christ, they said "Rejoice, and be exceedingly glad." They referenced a joyful reconciliation between God and humanity arriving in the person of Jesus the Christ. Most people think in terms of the birth of a child as being a joyful occasion, as an event of hope and renewal. Occasions such as births and marriage, and the return of a loved one from long journeys are occasions of great joy.

Christians also look forward to great joy in the form of reunion with loved ones in the resurrection described at the end of the Book of Revelation. The resurrection is described as a time when there are no more tears or suffering, a time when creation is renewed and humanity lives in peace and harmony in communion with God. Christ is understood as the One who brings reconciliation between humanity and God, and who first experienced resurrection, showing the way for others to follow.

Communion meditation can be thought of in terms of joyful reconciliation with God. Communion meditation can also be thought of in terms of participating in resurrection here and now, as we recognize and celebrate our own eternal Divine nature in Communion with God.

Christians of many denominations are familiar with the Sacrament of Holy Communion as an act of becoming close to Christ. For many, a great mystery takes place during Communion, and Christ actually becomes a part of who we are as individuals.

Christ Himself told us on multiple occasions that as human beings we are Divine in Nature. We are created in the image of God, and God is Divine. Christ was present with God at the beginnings of creation. Since we are the nondual accumulation of energy and matter that started with creation, we too were present at creation.

As humanity is created in God's Image, and as God's Being can be understood from a Trinitarian perspective, it's natural to understand our own human nature from a Trinitarian perspective as well. Just as God can be recognized as Father Divine Hopeful Consciousness, Jesus as Child Manifested Love, Mary Sophia as Mother Wisdom Faithfulness, and Spirit as life giving breath energy, so too human beings consist of these elements. In communing with God's Trinitarian Being, we begin to realize the essence of who we are as humans, Divinely wrought, and fearfully and wonderfully made.

Many Buddhists are familiar with a form of meditation known as Guru Yoga. In Guru Yoga, a Divine Being is identified and connected with. Some Buddhist sects recognize many Divine Beings, others identify no Divinity in particular.

As Christians, we have a very specific understanding of Divinity, and we have a specific Divine teacher, friend, and healer to connect with. We recognize Jesus the Christ as the Divine teacher, friend, and healer who is a nondual coexistent part of God and the Holy Spirit. Jesus the Christ, the Anointed One, is our Guru. We recognize Jesus the Christ as the One through whom we can connect with God the Father and the Holy Spirit. Jesus is the vine, Jesus is the door, Jesus is the Light. And so we focus on Jesus the Christ as we proceed in our Divine Communion.

We begin the process, like all others, with relaxed breathing. In and out, we recognize how it feels to have the air enter and leave our bodies. We remember that breath and spirit are closely associated in many cultures. The Chinese word Chi, the Greek word Pneuma, the Sanskrit word Prana, the Hebrew word Ruach, and the Tibetan word Lung, all mean breath and Spirit. We recognize the Holy Spirit as the Breath of God that brings life and healing.

As we relax, we picture Jesus in our minds. Our friend, our teacher, and our comforter, Jesus is the One who loves us unconditionally. Jesus may appear in robes, He may appear sitting in front of us or next to us, He may appear very close, comforting and embracing us. Jesus may appear as we have seen in pictures or artistic renditions, or Jesus may appear in a different form. Jesus may even appear in female form, if we need Jesus to. Some of us have been deeply hurt by men in our lives. Jesus understands, and Jesus will come to us in any form we need in order to share God's unconditional love.

Recognizing Jesus in our minds can be very difficult, or it can be very easy. This can be a very moving experience; we may feel such a wash of love and relief and joy that we may cry. We may lean into Jesus' arms and cry for as long as we need, Jesus is there for us. Its OK to cry. Its OK to let go.

Some of us may have difficulty visualizing Jesus. This is OK also. Jesus may appear to us in a vague form, difficult to recognize. Over time, as we relax and breath, we will become closer with Jesus. Jesus only comes as close as we can handle. Jesus is patient with us.

Once we are aware that we are not alone, that Jesus is present to guide us, we move forward in the process.

Step One: Communing with God's Consciousness

Communing with God comes in different forms for different people. For some, the experience is Baptismal, like water rising up to cleanse and heal. For others, the experience is Pentecostal, like tongues of fire touching our heads and cleansing and energizing us. For others, the experience of communing with God may come as gently as a breath, entering our bodies with every inhale, becoming a part of us, and cleansing and healing us. We may recognize that every exhale cleanses us further, releasing us from the afflictions that hold us back.

For the purpose of this phase in the tantric practice, we focus on breath as the means through which God communes with us. We are reminded that during the emptying phase we allowed our desires to pass from us. Ideally, our mind is clear moving into this phase. Being human, however, remnants of our desirous consciousness probably remain. This is OK. We are allowed to be ourselves. There is no judgment in this exercise, only hopeful, joyful, and peaceful progress.

We imagine the space that our mind occupies. We imagine with every breath that the Conscious Awareness of God the Father enters through our lungs, into our bloodstream, and fills our minds. Jesus is with us as we experience this, guiding us, comforting us. With every breath our mind becomes increasingly clear and open.

We may experience a wide variety of emotions while communing with God's Conscious Awareness. If we are fearful, we may choose to return to our breathing and relax, accepting the comforting embrace of Christ, embracing our inner child. If we are awed, we may do the same, or we may choose to continue to dwell here.

As our awareness increases, our consciousness expands, our sense of hopefulness expands as well. We begin to appreciate the breadth of God's Conscious Awareness as part of all that is. We may also begin to experience non-duality in its truest form, we are One. God's consciousness becomes a part of us, we become a part of God's consciousness. We are at peace, we are whole.

We are reminded that Jesus told us that the Kingdom of Heaven is within (Luke 17:21). We experience the Kingdom of Heaven as we embrace God's Conscious Awareness. Jesus told us that the Comforter / Advocate will teach and guide us (John 14:26). The Advocate brings God's Conscious Awareness into our minds. We are reminded that Jesus directed us to be perfect, even as God is perfect. In becoming a part of God's Consciousness, we are humbly obeying Jesus' commandments.

As we dwell within our minds, pure consciousness and peace fills us and expands throughout our being. In the book of Romans the apostle Paul reminds us that we can do all things through Christ who strengthens us (Phil 4:13). With every breath we take, Christ strengthens our minds, and fills our consciousness with God's Holy Presence.

In God's Holy Presence, we find our mind consciousness relaxing, accepting, simply Being. We recognize that we are a part of something much greater than ourselves, and that Divine Mystery is a part of us. There is hope and peace in knowing this. We relax and observe as the

Universe unfolds around us and through us. Just as Christ is wholly Human AND Wholly Divine, we recognize our own nondual existence, One with the Created Universe, One with the Creator God, and still uniquely ourselves.

In this state of peaceful Being, we find our thoughts returning to our breathing, centering us, grounding us. We reflect on our Divine Consciousness experience. Has this experience become part of our mind's "muscle memory," an integral part of us? Can we dwell within our Divine Consciousness for an extended period, or are we only glancing the Divine with our imaginations? Whatever we experience, we are kind to ourselves, we smile upon ourselves, we assure our selves that we can return to this state and practice for as long as it takes.

Step Two: Communing with Christ's Unconditional Love

Having found ourselves comfortable dwelling in Divine Consciousness, we turn our attention to our hearts. Whereas Divine Consciousness can be very awe inspiring, Love is close at hand and comforting.

We imagine the space where our heart resides.

We remember how during the self emptying phase we released our pain and resentments. During the Communion phase, we reverse the process, and our hearts are filled with Christ's healing unconditional love. We may imagine our hearts as empty bowls that are filled to over flowing with every breath we take. The Spirit is the vehicle through which love is carried, the Spirit is Love, and with every breath, our hearts are filled with love.

This experience can be very peaceful and satisfying, or it may be very emotional. Much of the time we thirst for unconditional love, sometimes we seek love in the wrong places. And instead of love, we sometimes find more emptiness and hurt.

Whereas human relationships often contain an element of hurt, God's love expressed in Christ never disappoints. The love that fills our hearts heals wounds and inspires us to love unconditionally as well. Christ's Divine love spills from our hearts and fills us with compassion. Divine Love is the well that doesn't just fill so that we thirst again, Divine love fulfills, satisfies, and brings peace.

As we experience this love, our thoughts may turn towards those who have hurt us and left resentful scars behind. We may find ourselves consciously forgiving them. Forgiveness is a Divine act of self healing. As if massaged with a soothing balm, the scars that mar our hearts are healing, and forgiving is a natural part of that process. We may even feel the beginnings of compassion towards those who have hurt us, and that's OK. But for now, we remain within our selves, accepting the healing as it comes. During the next phase of meditation, we will direct our compassion outwards. For now, we allow Christ's Divine Love to fill us and become a part of who we are, healing our hurts and washing away our resentments. We especially need to allow ourselves to love ourselves.

We are reminded of the characteristics of love that are described by Paul in 1 Corinthians 13. Love is patient, kind, gentle, never boastful, and always faithful. Love endures when all else passes away. And no matter who we are, or where we have been, or what we have done or endured in our lives, we are loved. We are loved completely and unconditionally. And all the hurts and wounds that have gone before telling us otherwise are washed away as our hearts are filled to overflowing.

As we rest within our hearts, as our sense of Divine Love grows, as our hearts brim with love and compassion, a warm sense of peace begins to envelope us. This peace comes from a growing sense of confidence and wisdom. Being filled with love, we take a compassionate look at our own journey, our pain, our emptiness, and our growing sense of healing. We recognize the losses we have experienced, and we may begin to understand the wisdom of acceptance. As Divine Love becomes an integral part of who we are, we recognize that suffering occurs, but love endures. Like pain endured while giving birth to a child, we recognize that suffering is a part of life, but suffering passes, and joy comes in the morning.

Christian thought often expresses Salvation in terms of accepting Jesus the Christ into our hearts. As we reflect on our acceptance of Christ's Divine Love, we recognize that in doing so we accept God's Salvation offered through Jesus the Christ.

Interlude: The Question of Humility

At this point, some part of us may be asking, but what of humility? Humility is after all a core value for Christians. In communing with and assimilating God's very nature, are we risking blasphemy?

This question is very important, and it goes to the heart of what it means to be humble, and what it means to hold a sense of self esteem. Questions about selflessness also arise. As Christians, we may feel called to be selfless and humble, servants and vessels to God through Christ, living lives of service and obedience.

The root of both the words humility and humanity is the Latin word Humus. Humus means earth, which suggests being grounded.

Many people misinterpret selflessness as a complete lack of self, and humility as a lack of self confidence. This misinterpretation is unhealthy and often leads to either self abuse or abuse at the hands of others. We know that a sense of self worth and self esteem is essential to living a healthy and fulfilled life. History is full of examples of people who control others by emphasizing selflessness and humility in the name of God while they themselves take advantage.

From one perspective, life can be viewed as a series of highs and lows, where a person soars and then is cut to the ground. Taken from this perspective, those moments on the ground are often viewed as humbling.

Tantric meditation, on the other hand, asks us to imagine a different perspective. Imagine being grounded and self aware much of the time, confident and at peace. This perspective aligns well with Sophia's Wisdom, as described in the biblical book of Ecclesiastes. This perspective also aligns well with the Gifts of the Spirit as described by Paul in his letter to the Galatians – love, kindness, gentleness, patience, faithfulness, self control – all "grounded" attributes, not affected by highs and lows.

So, instead of seeing humility in terms of "lack of self," for the purpose of Christian Tantric Meditation, humility can be seen as a "true understanding and appreciation of self." And because we are created in God's Image as revealed through Christ, we can understand ourselves as being both human and Divine.

In a sense, our Divine nature inspires humility. Our Divine nature demands that we act with love and compassion, toward ourselves and toward our fellow human beings, and toward all of creation.

In humility, we also acknowledge that although Communion with Divinity is offered freely to us, we cannot know the infinite depth of God's Mind, Love, and Faithful Wisdom. We can only know what God chooses to reveal to us. And we can be grateful for the Divine Gift of

God's Grace, as we experience it personally.

With all this in mind, we return ourselves to our centered breathing, and we are reminded that our mind, heart, and core chakras are free of desires, resentments, and fears. We are reminded that we have accepted the peace and the hopefulness associated with Divine Consciousness in our minds. We are reminded we have accepted Divine Unconditional Love into our hearts.

Step Three: *Communing with Mary-Sophia's Wisdom and Faith*

As human beings, we recognize that having faith can be challenging. When hard times come, our faith may fail. As our faith wanes, we may turn to the world to find comfort and fill the hole that is left behind with harmful behaviors. And many people who were raised in contact with communities of faith blame themselves for allowing their faith to slip. Many of us have been told that if we have enough faith, all our troubles will disappear. And we blame ourselves for being inadequate, for not having enough faith, for being human.

We are not at fault for having inadequate faith. We are not at fault for being human. Faith is a Divine attribute, and as Christians we believe that God has the ability to be truly faithful, but history and the bible shows over and over again that where God succeeds, humans struggle. As Christians we believe that the only human to ever hold true, unwavering faithfulness, was and is Jesus the Christ. We turn to Jesus to understand our true nature as nondual beings who are human and Divine in nature, even as Christ is human and Divine.

As we begin to embrace our own Divine nature, we also begin to embrace true faith. The Divine Consciousness and Divine Love we have embraced thus far in this tantric process leads us to Divine Faith, which is faith that does not, indeed can not waiver.

Along with faith, we begin to recognize a growing sense of wisdom within us. Wisdom recognizes that life has its ups and downs, but also recognizes through experience and faith that life goes on. Wisdom draws on faith to resist the temptation to over-react when life has its ups and downs. Wisdom recognizes that every experience we encounter holds meaning deeper than what we view on the surface, and patiently allows those deeper meanings to unfold.

We begin this step by imagining the space in which our core resides. We feel Divine Faithfulness grow with every breath we take. We feel Divine Wisdom becoming a part of our core being.

Without the burden of fear, including the fear of rejection and the fear of being criticized, our Divine Faithfulness grows. We remember rare moments of freedom when we were children, singing loudly in a bathroom and enjoying the naturally echoing sound, wildly applying crayon colors to a piece of paper or even a wall, spinning and spinning, dancing as if there were no gravity to weigh us down.

Our Divine sense of who we are, who we were created to be, begins to grow within us again. In a very real sense, we begin to experience a rebirth. We intentionally recognize the core chakra as the center of female Wisdom, the womb where new life grows in preparation for birth. In the gospel of John we are told that to experience true freedom, we must be born again. Within the confines of our core chakra, the process of rebirth begins.

The messages that we have received over the years telling us to stop dancing, stop singing, to stop drawing, are all washed away. As we accept the Divine Gift that God has given every last person among us, our faith in our self grows, even as our faith in God grows.

As we exhale, we continue to cleanse ourselves of our doubts, burdens and fears, and as we inhale, we continue to visualize God as Divine Mother becoming a part of our Core Being, and our own Divine nature revealed.

Through this process of tantric breathing and visualizing the space in which our core chakra resides, we may recognize the metaphysical makeup of ourselves that was discussed in the introduction of this text. We may feel Divine breath energy entering our body and riding through our central channels to fill our core. We may sense our central channel connecting our chakras, and our Divine Essence flowing through this channel.

Returning to our understanding of Guru Yoga, we may even get a sense of Jesus the Christ breathing on us, with the Holy Spirit emanating from His Presence, entering through our mouths and noses and flowing through our central channel to our core chakra, manifesting God as Divine Female.

Gratefully, peacefully, we continue to imagine the space where our Core chakra resides, and we dwell here. We are at peace, breathing, accepting, and faithful. We dwell here for as long as we are able, at first only a few minutes, but over time we learn to dwell here for longer. As our Divine sense of faith, wisdom, and self esteem grows, we sense that we are anchored, but not in a way that is a burden, rather in a way that is confident and resolute. Our core chakra anchors us, our sense of self develops. God is, We Are, We Exist in nondual relation with God as Hopeful Consciousness, as Unconditional Love, and as Faithful Wisdom, through Christ. Even as Christ is human and Divine, we too are human and Divine, as individuals and as part of all that is.

And our attention returns to our breathing. We center ourselves. We feel every breath in, every breath out. We feel our lungs filling, we feel our lungs emptying, and we are at peace.

Divine Communion Closing: Realizing our Divine Self

In the self emptying phase of this tantric practice, we were able to visualize our transparent selves rising from our core to encompass our entire bodies. As part of Divine Communion, we can visualize our Divine Self rising. We imagine the space in which our entire body resides.

Our sense of Divine Self may manifest in many forms. It may be similar to our transparent body, but composed of crystal or diamond. Our Divine Self may be filled with light, emanating outward from us. Our Divine Self may encompass the colors of the rainbow, and these colors may radiate from us, illuminating all that is around us.

As we rest within our Divine Self, we embrace the sense of peace that is a part of us. We accept the Divine presence of God through Christ, dwelling within us and centered in our chakras. We embrace a sense of wholeness as we accept our male and female aspects, in our consciousness, in our hearts, and within our core. We accept the Holy Spirit, coursing through us and restoring us with every breath.

We are reminded of the Guru Yoga practice that started this phase of our journey. We are reminded that Christ is near us, with us, guiding us, and embracing us. We smile at ourselves in contentment as we recognize Jesus the Christ smiling at us, loving us, and accepting us as sister and brother.

We are mindful of our surroundings, the ground that anchors us, the air that we breathe, the space surrounding us, and the nature outside our doors and windows. We are accepting of our place and our surroundings.

We are also mindful of our nondual nature as both human and Divine. We are eternal, and we are finite, and we can accept this with peace. We are individuals, and we are a part of God. We are individuals and we are part of the creation that surrounds us. We are individuals and we are a product of those who came before us.

We may find ourselves in a place where we experience an expanded sense of communion with others. As we rest in our Divine bodies, we may recognize the light that emanates from other Divine Beings as well. We may be reminded of Apostles and Saints who are a part of the Communion of Saints. We may be reminded of inspirational relatives or friends who are either still with us or have gone on before us. We may visualize the light from our own Divine Bodies joining the light from others as we participate in the Communion of Saints.

This experience of Divine Communion, like other experiences we have encountered, may be exhilarating, and it may be frightening. It may occur in a startling flash that interrupts our meditative experience. This is OK.

We return our attention to our centered breathing. We are grounded. In and out, we are mindful of our selves, the feeling of the air on our skin, in our nostrils and mouths, and in our lungs. We relax, and we smile.

STAGE THREE: OUTREACH COMPASSION

As you may have guessed by now, tantric meditation involves building upon previous experiences. Self emptying is a necessary prelude to Divine Communion, so that we can be open to receive Divine consciousness, love, and faithfulness. Similarly, Divine Communion is a necessary prelude to compassion meditation, as it opens channels with Divinity for Grace to work through us and beyond. After completing Divine Communion, there are several possible directions to proceed with Compassion Meditation.

Four manifestations of Compassion Meditation are presented here: compassion with self, compassion with loved ones, compassion with enemies, and finally universal compassion. Each manifestation is similar in practice, as each manifestation involves expanding consciousness, love, and faithfulness in an outward direction. Usually only one form of compassion is practiced in each meditative session, and it is recommended that compassion skills be developed in this order, first with self, then with loved ones, with enemies, and finally in a universal sense.

Like Divine Communion, compassion meditation is by nature relational. In Divine Communion we practice inviting and accepting God's Divine Presence into our being. Christian Scripture tells us that God desires this Divine Communion, and that Divine Communion was the purpose for Christ appearing on earth.

Notice that in Divine Communion, God does not force God's self into our consciousness. Also notice that God does not manifest as a puppet master, directing our actions and thoughts. Rather, God inspires us to fully become who we were created to be, hopeful, loving, faithful beings, each with our own unique gifts.

Similarly, the goal of compassion communion is not to control others. The roots of the word compassion suggest "suffering with", which tell us that the goal of compassion is to empathize with others. Whereas mindfulness has a goal of becoming self aware, compassion requires us to be aware and accepting of others. This can be very challenging, especially when we exercise compassion in relationship with people whom we consider enemies, or people who are culturally very different from ourselves.

In our practice of compassion, we strive to connect with elements that all humans have in common. In 1943, A. H. Maslow published "A Theory of Human Motivation", (MacLeod, 2007) which remains foundational in the understanding of human psychology today. Maslow's theory states that people take care of basic human needs, like food, shelter, and safety, before they become concerned with forming nurturing relationships. Likewise, people tend to fulfill relationship needs before they become concerned with building self esteem or reaching their highest potential.

If we think about our basic exercise of releasing the core fears that hold us back, we also recognize that the opposite of fear is a sense of faith and security. Every human being holds a mix of these elements. The process of releasing fears and allowing our faith and self confidence to grow is an exercise in fulfilling our basic safety needs. As we move forward with compassion meditation, we are reminded that everyone in the world holds some mix of fear and faith, and the balance of that mix helps determine how we interact with others.

If we think about our basic exercise of releasing resentments, we also recognize that the opposite of resentment is love. Again, every human being holds a mix of these elements. Releasing resentments and growing our ability to love unconditionally are exercises in fulfilling our relationship needs. As we move forward with compassion meditation, we are reminded that everyone in the world holds some mix of resentments and love for self and others, and the balance of that mix helps determine how we interact with others.

Finally, if we think about our basic exercise of releasing desires, we also recognize that the opposite of desire is freedom to experience joy and opportunity. Again, every human being holds a mix of these elements. Releasing desires and allowing ourselves to experience life to its fullest opens us to fulfilling our highest potential. As we move forward with compassion meditation, we are reminded that we and everyone else in the world hold some mix of self limiting desires and freedom to experience joy and opportunities, and the balance of that mix helps determine how we interact with others.

In 1 Corinthians 13, the Apostle Paul speaks of the gifts of faith, hope and love, the greatest of which is love. As Christians, we might also recognize a correlation between our need for security, love, and freedom with the gifts of faith, love, and hope. These gifts do not seek to control, but to liberate. As we reach out toward others in compassion, we also consciously recognize and share these gifts. This is the relational nature of compassion meditation, in which we seek to receive understanding and to share liberating unconditional hope, love, and faithfulness.

Practice 1: Compassion for Self

Whereas in previous meditation stages we worked to connect with our transparent and Divine selves, in self compassion we work to recognize and appreciate our human selves and the challenges we face as human beings. The practice of compassion for self involves revisiting desires, resentments, and fears that were identified during the self emptying process. However, rather than striving to release our desires, resentments, and fears, during compassion meditation we strive to simply recognize them and accept them. We also strive to recognize and accept our freedom, love, and strengths. Recognizing and accepting our human selves is a necessary precursor to recognizing and accepting the humanity in others when we direct our compassion outward.

Just as with the other stages of meditation, compassion begins in the mind chakra. We imagine the space where our mind resides. Instead of consciously releasing our desires and thoughts, we take a moment to reflect on them and accept them. We are aware of our desire for joy and freedom from suffering. We are aware that we hold this desire in common with all living beings.

Whether harmful or constructive, our desires are a part of who we are as humans. We are reminded that the first step in any healing process is accepting the challenges that are a part of our lives. As we peacefully acknowledge the desires we continue to hold, we find ourselves feeling kindness toward ourselves.

We also recognize the freedom that we enjoy. As we recognize the growth we have experienced in our freedom, we find our sense of hopefulness growing also. Our Divine Consciousness reaches with a sense of peace and understanding toward the desires and freedom that are a part of us.

We take time to dwell here, with our Divine Consciousness embracing our human consciousness, which includes our limitations and our potential. We might imagine our desires stemming from our inner child, who has needs that may not have been met when we were young. There may be some long standing empty spots in our lives that our desires strive to fill. Our inner child may be crying out for attention, for material comforts, or for some other form of stimulation to fill a gnawing void that we have had for as long as we can remember. In observing our own needs, our Divine Consciousness becomes all the more compassionate. We take a moment to embrace and comfort ourselves.

We may find that our inner child is not ready for comfort. We may find that our inner child rejects the peace and comfort that our Divine Consciousness has to offer. This is OK. We humbly accept ourselves for who we are and where we are at. Our Divine Consciousness is above all unconditionally accepting and patient. Even if we experience turmoil and pain, our Divine Consciousness, which remains in Communion with God, is at peace and hopeful.

As with other meditation stages, we may need to practice acceptance of our mind centered desires and freedom for several weeks before we feel comfortable. Journaling and consulting with friends or a minister or a counselor may be part of the process. The same will be true with every part of self compassion meditation.

Having taken time to observe and accept the desires and freedom that reside in our human consciousness, we move our attention to our heart, the seat of love. We imagine the space where our heart lies. We imagine the resentments that sit within our hearts. We visualize the hurts that we have suffered at the hands of others and even at our own hands. We recognize the love that we share as human beings, for ourselves and for others. As we observe both our resentments and the love we share, we allow our Divine sense of Unconditional Love, which exists in living communion with Jesus the Christ, to embrace the human hurts and loves we hold onto.

Again, our inner child may be at the seat of our hurts and resentments. While our Unconditionally Loving self may want to rush in and embrace our inner child, we also may recognize that our inner child is not ready to receive such an all encompassing love. Our inner child may even view love as something that is smothering and controlling rather than comforting and liberating. Respectfully, we offer ourselves the room we need to feel safe. We observe our resentments and we accept them. We recognize that our hurts and resentments are a part of who we are as humans. They have been a part of us for a long time, and we respect our need for them and the role they play in our humanity.

We also observe and respect the human love that we hold and share with others. When we think of love, we may think of friends and family, we may think of our relationship with God through Christ, and we may even think of ourselves. Even though the human love we hold may be imperfect and full of conditions and attachments, it is real, and we can appreciate that. Despite all of the hurts and challenges we have endured, love lives on within us. This is humbling and endearing.

We may find that we harbor resentments toward ourselves. We have all suffered losses and failures in our lives. Most of us have experienced hurting ourselves and others as well, either through ignorance or intent. While we hope for forgiveness, we recognize that we may not be ready to forgive ourselves. And yet, in spite of all this, love exists and remains a part of us. The hurts and resentments exist, but so does love. When we are ready to forgive ourselves, our Divine Love Self will be ready with open arms to accept our humanity, even as the Christ with whom we are in loving communion stands ready to accept us.

We are reminded of our nondual nature. We are unique, and we are a product of creation and our environments. Our childhood experiences, our genetic makeup, our friends, our enemies, the food we have eaten, the things we have done, are all a part of us. We are not self existent, we are a product of many factors, and we have been materially in existence since the beginning of creation. This knowledge allows us to give ourselves some room to forgive. Influences that we have no control over have been shaping us since the beginning of time. We may resent some of these influences, and knowledge of this helps our Divine Selves to grow in compassion and understanding.

After mindfully accepting our human resentments and love, we turn to our core. We imagine the space where our core resides. Here is where our Divine Female resides, source of wisdom and faith. We recognize the human fears that reside deep within the core of our being. We recognize the core sense of faith, security, and strength that we also hold deep within ourselves. We mindfully observe our fears and strengths, and accept them as part of who we are.

As we look at our core fears, we may recognize our inner child, who carries fears that have been a part of us for a long time. While our Divine Female nurturing self may want to rush in and comfort our inner child and provide reassurance that we are safe, we may need to maintain a respectful distance. These fears have been a part of us for a long time, and we may not be ready to part with them. By observing ourselves and our human fears, our sense of compassion and love for our humanity grows.

We also recognize our core strengths that have developed over the years. Our Divine selves recognize the accomplishments we have enjoyed and challenges we have overcome to this point in our lives. As we look at both our fears and our strengths coexisting within us, we recognize a growing sense of respect for ourselves. We are human and imperfect, and yet we are strong and resilient.

Later, in day to day life, we may encounter an object or experience that stimulates fear. When that occurs, we may also remember this meditative experience of observing our fears and our strength from the perspective of Divine Faith. We may smile at ourselves in acceptance and understanding when this occurs. But for now, our Divine Selves simply re-assure us that we have overcome challenges before, and that we will continue to let go of fears and grow in security and confidence. God the Comforter, Mary Sophia, is with us in Divine Communion, and ready to help us when we are ready to accept help and reassurance.

It may take several weeks of practice to become comfortable with accepting our fears and strengths. Even if we explore other forms of compassion meditation, we recognize that we need to be comfortable with self compassion before moving on in earnest. We utilize our journaling, friends, and counselors to help us move through the process.

Having moved through our chakras with respect and compassion, we are reminded how we have, in previous sessions, practiced visualizing our transparent selves and our Divine Selves rising. For the purpose of this exercise, we visualize our whole human self rising. We imagine the space in which our whole human being resides. We recognize and accept ourselves for who we are as humans, with all our desires and freedom, resentments and love, and fears and strength. We allow ourselves the space to just be – who we are, where we are. No pressure to change or fix or feel. We just are.

As we dwell within our human selves, our sense of compassion for our self grows as well. We recognize that for all our flaws and weaknesses, we are beautiful. We accept our self unconditionally. We love our self unconditionally. We respect our self unconditionally.

We eventually sense our human self growing in Communion with our Divine self. We are reminded that our Divine Self is in Communion with God, through Christ, in Hopeful Consciousness, in Love, and in Faithful Wisdom.

We also sense our human/Divine selves growing in Communion with our transparent self. Experiencing this multidimensional Triune Communion – Human self, Divine Self, and Transparent self, each with Mind, Heart, and Core, brings us a sense of wholeness and peace. We are reminded that we are made in the image of God, as Creator Divine Parent, human child Christ, and invisible Female Spirit. Even as God is "I Am", we can comfortably acknowledge that "We Are", complete and at peace.

Gradually, we return our attention to our breathing. Our breathing grounds us, it centers us, it cleanses us. With a sense of peace and acceptance, we open our eyes and we smile.

Practice 2: Compassion for Loved Ones

In experiencing the "Compassion for Self" practice, the basic process for compassion meditation was revealed. In self compassion meditation, a great deal of emphasis was placed on not judging nor controlling. Instead emphasis was placed on accepting and comforting. This will be especially important when shifting attention outward, away from self.

Until now, all focus has been on self, which has been a necessary foundation for moving our attention outward. Just as we have ideas about what is right and good and healthy for ourselves, as human beings we project those same ideas onto others. Common family discussions include "if only you would go on a diet, stop smoking, etc, etc, you would experience some relief from your suffering." Sometimes people we love refuse to visit doctors or follow prescribed treatments, sometimes they refuse to even listen. This can be frustrating.

If it's hard to accept that suffering is part of life for ourselves, its doubly hard to accept suffering as a part of life for people we love. No one wants to see loved ones suffer, but apart from triage activities like helping people get food, shelter, and medical care they need, we cannot compel anyone to accept our best intentions. Beyond triage, the most we can give anyone is unconditional acceptance of them and their suffering. Once again we are reminded that compassion means "suffering with," not controlling.

A major part of maintaining healthy relationships with people, including people we love, is maintaining healthy boundaries. Relationships that are overly entwined with each other tend to be unhealthy. Nondual principles are especially important to remember in relationships. In a marriage or intimate partnership, this would translate as "S/he is my spouse/partner, AND S/he is her/his own person." Sometimes this can be hard to remember, because our human love gets confused with our desire and attachment to the "Other."

This is especially important to remember when engaging in compassion meditation. In applying the space oriented projection technique to extending ourselves outward, we must think of our projection in terms of visiting a church of another denomination or even a sacred temple of a different tradition. The person we share our compassion with is as Sacred and Divine as we are, whether they are aware of it or not. God in Christ is with them, whether they are aware of it or not, and whether we can recognize God's presence in their outward lives or not.

Christianity teaches us that our bodies are sacred temples, and when we reach out to others in compassion, we reach out to sacred temples of Divine Presence. Just as we do not appreciate people barging into our own churches and demanding changes, Others do not appreciate being controlled, even and especially if they are suffering.

This is also a good place to be reminded of the principle of equanimity. In the presence of Infinite Love, we are all loved equally. Mathematically, the number one billion is no closer to infinity than the number zero. In Christian language, we all fall short of the Glory of God, but we are saved by Grace through Christ's perfect faith, which demonstrates God's Unconditional Love for all people and all of creation.

This point needs to be reiterated because it is so important. In the presence of Unconditional Love, everyone is loved, without condition. While we are all loved equally, we are not all the same, we are different people, and we all have different ways of expressing ourselves.

With all this in mind, we return to our centered breathing and relax. Ideally, we have completed the Self Emptying and Divine Communion exercises, which means we are transparent and in touch with our inner Divinity. We are at peace, our breath energy flows with the faith, love, and hope and that emanates from our chakra centers.

We imagine the space that our loved one occupies. We imagine the location of their conscious awareness. With every exhaled breath we reach out of our own being toward the Other, the one with whom we wish to share our compassion. With every inhaled breath, we open ourselves up to the conscious experiences of the Other.

As we contemplate the mind of the Other, we are reminded that they have desires, some that they may know about, many that they do not know about. We are aware that all people possess an innate desire to be joyful and free from suffering. We are also reminded that the Other also enjoys some sense of personal freedom.

We are reminded of our own desires, and how our desires contribute to our own suffering. We allow our own Divine Consciousness to recognize and peacefully accept the desires and freedom within the Other. Our understanding of what motivates the Other may grow. We may even recognize an inner child within the other.

With every inhale, we open ourselves to the desires and freedom of the other. We are reminded of our own Divine Consciousness existing in Communion with God. With every exhale, we allow our own Divine Consciousness to reach out towards the Other. Whether God's Divine presence is recognized or accepted by the Other does not matter. We respect the relationship the Other has with Divinity, in whatever form it takes. All that matters is that we are present, we accept, and we care.

We may dwell with our thoughts directed towards the space that the Other's mind occupies for several minutes. As we dwell here, we gain a greater and greater appreciation for the desires and freedom that motivate the Other. Even as we learn to accept and appreciate our own humanity, we grow in acceptance and humility in the presence of the Other's humanity. The Other is a created Being, just as we are, with unique gifts, hopes, dreams, and burdens. We respect the Other's potential and the burdens the Other carries.

After sharing Divine Consciousness for several minutes, our attention shifts to the heart of the Other. Can we imagine the space that the Other's heart occupies? We recognize that they have resentments and hurts in their lives, just as we do. We also recognize that they have love within their hearts, for themselves and for others.

We do not know the specific hurts that are a part of them, or the scars that they carry. There may even be resentments towards us, for hurts that we have left behind, whether intentionally or not. We recognize the fragility of the human heart, how easily it can be hurt and how much time it takes to heal. We respect the pain the Other has endured, and we accept the Other for who they are and where they are at. We recognize their suffering and their love as sacred, even as Christ's love and suffering and our own love and suffering are sacred.

With every inhaled breath, we become more sensitive to the resentments and love that the Other carries. We are reminded of our own sacred communion with Christ, and the unconditional love that Christ pours into our hearts. With every exhaled breath, we visualize this unconditional love pouring out towards the Other. This love may be accepted, it may be rejected, it may be recognized, or it may not. None of this matters. All that matters is that we are present and we love. We do not wish to control in any way, we simply love. We simply breathe. We simply are.

At peace, we move our attention toward the core of the Other. We imagine the space that the Other's core occupies. We recognize that the Other has fears and strength just as we do. We recognize that fears and their strength help shape who the Other is. We cannot know the nature of those fears or strengths, even as we may not fully appreciate the nature of our own deep seated fears nor the depths of our own strengths until they are tested. But just the fact that they have fears and strengths draws out our compassion.

We may recognize our own Divine Mother consciousness rising to comfort the inner child of the Other. This is natural. When we recognize fear in a child, we wish to provide comfort. But we also recognize the sacred autonomy of the Other. We recognize that the person we feel compassion for may be protecting her or his inner child from further pain and fear. We respect the Other's desire to protect self, and the energy devoted to protecting self, even as we devote energy to enforcing our own healthy boundaries.

With every inhaled breath, we become more sensitive to the fears and strength the Other carries. We recognize the wisdom and faith that originates with God as female Mary Sophia, and communes with our own inner core Divinity. With every exhale, we share our Divine wisdom-faith with the Other. We recognize that the Other may reject the wisdom-faith we share on their behalf. This is OK. We respect the personhood of the Other, the core of her/his own sacred temple. We do not wish to control, we simply are. Breathing in and out, our Core wisdom-faithfulness recognizes the Other's humanity. We smile.

At this point, we may choose to close our compassion practice and return our focus to our breathing. Or, our attention may turn to a particular burden the Other carries that we may be aware of. This burden may be physical in nature, and it may be located in a specific space within the body of the Other. Because we hold great affection for this Other, it may be very difficult for us to accept the suffering that this burden causes the Other. This burden may be as simple as a common cold, or as devastating as addiction or cancer. Whatever the affliction is, we feel called to reach out in compassion in a special way.

Can we recognize the space that this burden occupies? Can we recognize the suffering that the Other carries? This suffering may be too much for us to even imagine, so at any point we may choose to return our attention to our own breathing. This is OK. If we choose, we may accept the suffering within the Other for what it is, a part of that person that we have no control over.

We may recall an experience of sitting with a loved one in a hospital room or nursing home. We recognize that while suffering is a part of the Other's reality, simply being present can bring comfort, to them as well as to ourselves. With every breath we inhale we recognize the suffering the Other endures, and with every exhale we direct our Divine hope, love, and faithfulness towards the space occupied by the Other's affliction. We surrender control to the Divine, to Christ's healing presence, for this is all we can do. We find peace.

Gently, we return our attention to ourselves. We breathe in healing awareness, we exhale our own desires. We breathe in Divine Love, we breathe out resentments. We breathe in faithfulness, we breathe out fear and pain. We ground ourselves within ourselves, we again recognize our Divine Selves in communion with God as Father, Child, and Mother. We may dwell here within ourselves for several minutes, at peace, allowing ourselves Hope, Love, and Faith.

We are reminded that we are whole beings. We take a moment to allow our transparent self to commune with our Divine Self, and our Transparent/Divine Selves to commune with our human self. We feel whole and restored.

We return our attention to our breathing. In and out, we feel our breath in our nose and mouth, filling and emptying our lungs, expanding and releasing our diaphragms. We are fully present and aware of our self and our surroundings. Gently, we open our eyes. We smile. We accept. We simply are.

Later, when we encounter our loved one physically, we may experience a new sense of peace and acceptance within our self. Our loved ones will likely notice a change in our attitudes. Whereas we may have been anxious and perhaps even invasive or controlling in the past, we find we are more at peace and accepting. We find we are more able to simply be with the Other, enjoying their presence, sharing the concerns and issues they choose to share with us.

We might even find increasing openness and intimacy with those we love. They may choose to share more and draw closer to us. Just as we tend to open up toward people who accept us for who we are, we may find others opening up to us more as well. Whereas people tend to draw away from others who say "you should," people tend to trust others who are able to just listen and accept unconditionally. And sometimes, we may even find ourselves participating in the healing of the Other. Healing comes from unconditional acceptance and love. If we are blessed with this experience, we are further humbled for being allowed to observe and participate.

This change in relationship and experience may or may not occur. If it does not, we are able to accept that as well. Each person's relationship with God is unique, and healing comes in its own time and space within that unique relationship. By simply being and accepting and loving unconditionally, we do the most we can for the Other, and we humbly accept that.

Practice 3: Compassion for Enemies

Having practiced compassion for self and compassion for loved ones, we may feel ready to accept the challenge of directing our consciousness towards someone who has hurt us in the past or is hurting us in the present. This Other with whom we have a negative relationship may be near or far. This may be an authority figure we have a working relationship with, or an acquaintance or relative who has been a hurtful presence in our lives. The Other may or may not even be physically alive at this point.

Whereas healthy boundaries with loved ones are important, healthy boundaries are extremely important when practicing compassion for enemies. This is a good time to examine our motivation for having compassion for enemies. If we have had negative experiences that continue to affect us years after the events, we may need to forgive and let go in order to move on with our lives. Compassion meditation can help with this.

The purpose of compassion meditation is not to change someone else. The purpose of compassion meditation is to change ourselves, to build our acceptance and unconditional love for others. While its true that many relationships improve if one member of a relationship practices compassion and unconditional love, the goal of compassion meditation is not to change others.

In fact, the reaction of others to compassion practice may turn out to be the opposite of what we hope or intend. For example, if an abusive individual practices compassion meditation with an abused partner in mind, the victim's response may be to finally develop enough self love to separate herself/himself from the abuser. The purpose of compassion meditation, for self and for others, is not to control, but to liberate.

If we are currently in an abusive relationship, one in which we are either the abuser or the abused, then we may be hoping to end the abuse by exercising compassion. This may be possible, but we need to remember the importance of safety. When actively engaged in an abusive relationship, basic needs must be attended to first. Safety is first and foremost. People who are engaged in chronically abusive relationships need to develop plans for maintaining physical and emotional safety and well being for themselves and others who are affected by those relationships, including children and elderly family members.

Codependence is an affliction where people come to believe that they can control others by being "nice" or "compassionate." These attempts at being "nice", whether made by abusers or victims, always lead back into a cycle of abuse that gets worse and worse over time.

If we find ourselves actively involved in a codependent relationship, serious work needs to be done on self compassion before moving forward with practicing compassion for loved ones or enemies. When we have self compassion, we find the strength to establish adequate boundaries to protect ourselves from abusive individuals and situations.

As we develop self awareness, we may discover that our "compassion for loved one" meditation is really being directed towards an abusive or an abused person in a codependent relationship. In many codependent relationships, the line between love and abuse, and who the abuser and who the abused are, gets blurry as the cycle of abuse spins more and more out of control.

A good test for identifying whether a relationship is codependent is to catch one's self thinking "if only s/he would change, life would be better." This thinking provides a warning sign that we believe our well being is controlled by another.

Sometimes Christians believe that we have the "right" interpretation of scripture and we feel that we "know" God's Word. We may also feel responsibility for "asserting" God's Word on others, especially loved ones, so that others might avoid "eternal damnation." We might equate "losing control" of others with surrendering them to the control of evil forces. In fact, the opposite is true. Surrendering control of others allows them to establish their own relationship with God, in their own time and in their own way.

Once control is surrendered, the Other may drift away from church, or even develop what we view as destructive behaviors. The Other may form new relationships with people who are hurtful in some way. If this occurs, we may need to accept that suffering is part of who the "Other" is for now, driven by their own desires, resentments, and fears. We may recognize this while practicing compassion meditation and we may even find ourselves better able to accept them for who they are. And once we accept Others for who they are, true healing and liberation can begin, for ourselves and for the Others.

With all of this in mind, after briefly moving through the self emptying and communion meditation stages, we find ourselves in our meditative postures, breathing in and out. With every breath, we find ourselves more deeply grounded, connected with the earth and at peace. We are aware of our environment and our bodies, the air we breathe and the way expanding our lungs feels. We are aware of our Divine Being, which is connected with God, in mind, heart, and in our core. God dwells in Christ, and Christ Dwells in us, and we are eternal and overflowing with hope, love, and faith.

The process starts by imagining the space that the Other occupies. If we don't know where the Other is located, we may imagine a space in the general direction we last encountered them. Even if the Other is deceased, we can remember the location of an encounter with them while they were alive. We imagine the space where the mind of the Other resides.

Using our Divine mind, we think about the desires that drive the Other, even the desires that drive the Other to be in conflict with us. We are aware that the Other, like all people, desires joy and freedom from suffering. We may be surprised to find that the desires and the freedom experienced by the Other are not so different from our own. We may even find that the similarity between our desires and freedom help fuel the conflict we experience.

As we direct our Divine Consciousness towards the mind of the Other, we breathe, slowly, in and out. We share the peaceful awareness of our Divine mind with the Other, the peaceful awareness of God who resides within us. We find ourselves accepting the Other, even as God accepts us and the Other, with all our desires and freedom. We recognize equanimity between our self and the Other. Even though we may be at odds, we are loved equally in the presence of Divinity. As we inhale, we increase our awareness of the desires and freedom that the Other holds, and as we exhale, we share our Divine hope for freedom with the Other.

Whether the Other is aware of or accepts our peaceful intentions or not is immaterial. The peaceful awareness we cultivate remains within our self. The peace we cultivate inspires our acceptance of the Other, and in accepting the Other, we are changed. We realize that although we cannot change the Other, by changing our self we change the relationship between us. We wish the other well, and we continue to breathe mindfully, grounded within our self.

After some period of time, our attention turns to the heart of the Other. Can we imagine the space that the Other's heart occupies? Slowly, purposefully, we breathe in and out, grounded within ourselves and extending our Divine Love towards the Other.

The resentments and the love that the Other harbors enters and touches our heart. Some of that resentment or love may be directed toward us. This gives us pause as we realize that we may be a source of pain for the Other, whether we intend to be or not. We also humbly recognize that we cannot know most of the resentments and love that reside within the Other, even as we may not be fully aware of the sources of our own resentments and love. We respect the scars the Other bears, the pain the Other endures day to day. Our acceptance and respect for the Other's pain and love inspires compassion in us. We begin to understand the feelings the Other experiences, as we too carry resentment and love.

With every inhaled breath, we become more aware of the resentments and love the Other holds in his or her heart. We recognize Christ's Divine Healing Love that resides in our hearts, and with every exhaled breath we share that Love with the Other. We recognize that the breath that connects us is our Divine Essence, our Chi, in Communion with the Holy Spirit.

We also understand that whether or not the Other recognizes or accepts our loving intentions is immaterial. We strive to accept the Other for who they are and where they are at, unconditionally, even as God accepts the Other unconditionally. In so doing we are changed, our attitude changes, and the relationship between us and the Other changes.

As we mindfully return to our breathing, grounded within ourselves and connected with the Other, we shift our thoughts to the core of the Other. Can we imagine the space that the Other's core occupies? Can we imagine the fears and strengths that the Other harbors?

We recognize that the Other is motivated by fears and fortified by strengths in the same way that we are. Fear is the core emotion that motivates fight or flight behavior. As we contemplate the fears of this Other person with whom we are in conflict, we recognize that our conflict may originate from both the fears we hold and the fears that the Other holds. The Other may react to his or her fears in a manner that is passive, or aggressive, or even passive-aggressive. Similarly, we may need to humbly confess that we too have demonstrated these same behaviors in conflict.

The idea of equanimity is very important here, because aggressors are often identified as the "bad person" in conflict situations, while passive people are identified as "victims." Both aggressive and passive behaviors can be harmful, and both stem from basically the same source, fear. Both behaviors, passive and aggressive, are most likely learned and carried over from childhood experiences.

As we recognize the fears and strengths that the Other holds as well as our own fears and strengths, our sense of compassion grows. We continue maintaining respectful boundaries with the other, especially when safety may be an issue. But we realize it is very possible to maintain safe boundaries and still feel compassion for the Other.

With every inhale, we grow in awareness and acceptance of the Other's fears and strengths. We experience God's wise and faithful Female presence filling us, and with every exhale we share our compassion and faith with the Other. We may even recognize the inner child of the Other self isolating or reacting with aggressiveness. This grows our compassion even further, as we maintain safe and respectful boundaries.

After practicing compassion with the core of the Other, we begin to recognize and appreciate the whole human being with whom we share our compassion. Just as we have witnessed the rising of our own Divine and Human selves, we recognize the presence of the Other's Divine and Human selves. We appreciate the inner Divinity that the other holds in communion with their own inner humanity.

After some time, we return our thoughts to our own humanity, our own Divinity, our own being. We breathe. We experience restoration. We remember that Divinity dwells within us, as God is present in our mind, Christ is present in our heart, and Mary Sophia is present within our core. With every breath, we accept Healing Grace in the Holy Spirit.

We recognize that sharing compassion with enemies can be difficult, stressful, even painful, and we congratulate ourselves for the effort. Whether we feel satisfied with our efforts or continue to harbor some resentment or fear towards the Other, this is OK. We find solace in knowing we can continue this practice for as long as we feel necessary.

We are reminded again that we are whole beings. We take a moment to allow our transparent selves to commune with our Divine Selves, and our transparent/Divine Selves to commune with our human selves. We feel whole and restored.

We return our attention to our breathing. In and out, we feel our breath in our nose and mouth, filling and emptying our lungs, opening and releasing our diaphragm. We are fully present and aware of ourselves and our surroundings. Gently, we open our eyes. We smile. We accept. We simply are.

Later, if we encounter this person with whom we are in conflict, we may find we are more at peace and accepting. The Other may notice our change, and may react positively or even more negatively. Either way, our ability to maintain healthy boundaries is strengthened. We can recognize the challenges and strengths that motivate the Other, and we can respect the Other's desire for joy and freedom from suffering, the Other's desire for love, and the Other's desire for safety.

It may be obvious by now that compassion meditation is also a form of communion meditation. We recognize that even though we practice Communion with Divinity, we cannot completely know the Mind, Heart, and Core of God. We can only know God to the extent that God chooses to reveal God's self to us. We also recognize that when we offer compassion toward another, we cannot know the mind, heart, and core of the Other, and we have no control over whether the Other is aware of or accepts our compassion.

In the same sense that compassion meditation can be extended toward friends or enemies, compassion meditation can also be directed toward groups of people considered friendly or hostile. Utilizing compassion meditation in a way that recognizes groups of people who have different political or religious or cultural views and values can be very helpful. Compassion meditation directed toward groups of people can be practiced in much the same way as compassion meditation practiced with individual friends or enemies in mind.

Practice 4: Universal Compassion

Universal compassion is utilized in a more generic manner than previous compassion practices. Universal compassion meditation can be shared with all of humanity and beyond, with all sentient beings, all living creatures, and all of creation.

In the traditional tantric sense, compassion is often practiced at a universal rather than a personal level. As Christians, we look forward to a time when universal healing is realized, and God's ultimate plan for all of creation comes to fruition. Similarly, many Buddhists feel that we are called to aid in the liberation of all beings from the cycle of suffering. Until every being is liberated from suffering, we all continue to suffer in some sense. We are after all a human family, a family of creation, and there is a reason we were given the Divine gift of compassion toward others, human and otherwise.

For the purpose of this exercise, geographically expanding universal compassion will be illustrated, directed outward in an ever greater radius toward all of humanity, all sentient beings, all living creatures, and all of Creation.

As with other compassion meditative practices, we pick up where Divine communion leaves off. We are centered, breathing, and grounded. We are aware of our transparent self, our indwelling Divinity, and our human self that possess both desires and freedom, resentments and love, and fear and security.

We imagine the space that our room occupies. We imagine the space that our dwelling occupies. We imagine the area of our local municipality. We imagine all of the people within the space that our local municipality occupies.

As we recognize the existence and relative positions of all of these people, we may think of them as glowing Beings, both Human and Divine, finite and Eternal. We recognize they have a wide variety of desires and freedom, resentments and love, and fears and strength, even as we share these attributes. The common humanity that we share moves us to compassion for them. Our own Divine senses of Hope, Love, and Faith expand. Our Divine Self expands to encompass our radius of compassion.

We are reminded that all beings share a mix of desires and joyful freedom. As we contemplate the consciousness of all the beings we encounter, we recognize that the proportions of the mix vary from person to person. Some people seem very driven, others seem very detached and free-spirited, but most people exist somewhere between the extremes of all consuming desire and complete unattached freedom. As we recognize the commonality of our desires for joy and freedom from suffering, we are moved to compassion. We suffer with the others, and we rejoice with the others. We recognize our human self reflected in the others.

Similarly, we are reminded that all beings share a mix of resentments and love. As we contemplate the hearts of all the beings we encounter, we recognize that the proportions of the mix vary from person to person. Some people are very focused on themselves, gathering relationships and objects and behaviors that they think will fulfill or bring them meaning. As they realize that self focus does not foster endearment or fulfillment, feelings of hurt and resentment arise. Other people are very altruistically outwardly focused, spending their time and resources sharing and giving to the greatest extent possible. Even the most altruistic individual feels hurt and resentment when sharing is rejected or abused. Most people exist somewhere in the continuum between resentful self focus and altruistic "other" focus. We recognize our own human hearts reflected in this continuum in every other person we encounter, and we are moved to compassion..

Finally, we are reminded that all beings share a mixture of fear and security. As we contemplate the cores of all the beings we encounter, we recognize that the proportions of the mix vary from person to person. Some people act out in extremes, either passively hiding away or aggressively in an attempt to control their fears. Other people appear very self confident and comfortable with themselves and others. But even the most self confident person harbors some fears within, including fears associated with the core human needs of food, shelter, and safety. Most people live somewhere in the continuum between fear and security, and we recognize our human connection in this continuum. We are moved to compassion towards those who suffer from fear, and for those who enjoy a sense of security and well being.

As we expand our consciousness to encompass more and more of creation, we may begin to feel confused or disoriented. If this happens, we return to our grounded breathing, here and now. We are free to end this practice at any time. If we feel comfortable, we may choose to expand our consciousness further. We imagine the space occupied by the state/province we are part of. We imagine the space occupied by our nation. Our continent.

More and more sentient beings, points of light enter our awareness. The breadth of both the joy and the suffering endured by these beings reflects in us. We remember our sense of being transparent, and we are able to observe without being overwhelmed. We can be a part of it all and separate. We are nondual beings with an ever widening consciousness.

Once again, if we feel disoriented we may choose to return to our breathing centered selves. Or we may choose to expand farther. We imagine the space that the planet earth occupies. We imagine the light of every sentient being. Every living being. Every animal, every plant, every microbe that shares the Divine breath of life.

Breathing gently, we smile. We are at peace. Divine Hope, Love, and Faith flows through us and blankets the entirety of creation. We are one and we are part of the whole.

Expanding even farther, we imagine the space occupied by our solar system, and then our galaxy. Like the stars that comprise it, the galaxy glows with life, hope, love, and faithfulness. We realize that the star systems within our galaxy include planets, and some of those planets include life, and among those that include life, some may include sentient life. Like us, those sentient beings are hopeful, loving, and faithful. Like us, they are subject to joy and suffering. Like us, they are finite and eternal.

Finally, we may choose to imagine the space that the entire Universe occupies. The galaxies glow with the light of life, hope, love, and faithfulness. We are at peace, and the gifts of the Spirit flow through and join all living creatures, all sentient beings, throughout all galaxies. We are in true loving communion with creation and Divinity, with all sentient beings, whatever form they might have. We are aware of our own individuality, glowing with our own humanity and Divinity, and we are a part of the whole of creation.

During any point in this exercise, we may become aware that we are not alone in reaching out in Divine Communion with Others. We may also become aware that Divinity also reaches through Other beings toward us. We are part of a network of sentient beings, all reaching out, all sharing, all connected, through and with Divine being.

Just as our Guru Yoga experience with Jesus the Christ may have been emotional, connecting with other beings on such a scale may evoke emotions as well. We know we are not alone, we know that we are in loving communion with Divinity through Christ, but we sometimes forget that Others also reach out in Loving Communion toward us, and we can gain strength and hope from that experience. We recognize these other beings as saints, enlightened ones, and beloved companions.

Smiling, peaceful, we dwell here in communion with hopeful joy, love, and faithful security. And gently, peacefully, we return to our own self awareness, our own breathing. We are grounded, we are whole, we are loved. We are transparent, we are Divine, we are human. We are whole. We feel air entering and leaving our nostrils. We feel our lungs and our diaphragms expanding and releasing. We smile. We open our eyes.

Compassion Postlude: Living Compassion

After practicing compassion meditation in its various forms, in our day to day lives we recognize ourselves living out our human freedom and desires, love and resentments, and strength and fears. Whereas previously we may have found ourselves reacting to certain situations impulsively, with anger or fear or other emotions, we may find now that we take a moment to contemplate our emotions and impulses prior to reacting. Instead of reacting, we may find ourselves smiling at our own rising self awareness, acknowledging our humanity, and moving forward.

While we retain healthy goals, we recognize the desires that drive us, and rather than letting those desires dictate our behaviors, we give ourselves space to allow opportunities to arise. While retaining healthy boundaries, we recognize resentments that drive us, and rather than letting those resentments dictate our behaviors, we allow ourselves to love unconditionally, in a way that is free of attachments. While retaining a healthy sense of self care and preservation, we recognize the fears that hold us back and cause us to react irrationally, and we give ourselves space to let go and experience growing self esteem and self confidence.

Similarly, after compassion meditation, we encounter others, people we love, people we dislike, and people we don't even know. We recognize within Others the common humanity that we all share. We may give the people we love more space to grow and experience life, choosing to support rather than control, letting go of attachment in lieu of unconditional love.

We may recognize attributes of people we don't care for within ourselves. This may motivate us to be more accepting and hopeful for their well being, while maintaining healthy boundaries.

We may also feel more comfortable and accepting of people we don't know, especially people from other cultures and backgrounds. We may find ourselves forming friendships with people we never before imagined possible.

The awareness we gather while practicing Christian Tantric Meditation stays with us as we live our lives and encounter others. Whether simply breathing deeply when encountering stress, or feeling the peace of knowing that Christ dwells within us, or experiencing compassion when encountering others, the awareness we gather becomes a part of us.

MEDITATION AND BALANCE

By now we have at least read through all the meditation exercises provided in this guide, from introductory breathing and space oriented projection, through self emptying, Divine Communion, and the various manifestations of compassion. We may feel comfortable with and have a sense of assimilating some of the practices, and we may still be working towards being comfortable with other practices.

We may be asking ourselves, with all these options, how should we practice? At first practice is all about learning individual stages and developing a "muscle memory" for each, so that they become a part of us. But what about after we have developed some comfort with each of the stages?

One can never "perfect" meditation, there are always more ways to grow, and there is always more to learn. And every time we practice, from the most rudimentary introductory exercises to universal compassion, we grow.

Outside of the meditative practice, we see our patience and relationships growing stronger, deeper. We find our work environments more rewarding. We also recognize opportunities arising that our own desires had been blocking for years.

We also recognize areas where we need growth. Some resentments, for example, have a habit of popping back up from time to time, even when we feel we have let them go completely. We may notice some unhealthy desires occupying our mind when we feel stressed. We may also recognize fear in situations that we hadn't recognized previously.

Do we need to practice meditation every day? Some people would say yes. Others feel they need to take a break from time to time, especially if they need to process strong feelings that have arisen during meditation. Taking counsel from a friend, a minister, or a professional may be considered as well.

One may choose to develop a sense of discipline while meditating. Discipline may vary significantly from person to person. One person may choose to meditate every other day, another may choose to meditate multiple times per day for shorter periods.

Whatever frequency of meditation is chosen, it's important to maintain a sense of balance in meditation practice as well as in life. For example, in meditation, a person may choose to cycle through all the practices and then start over again with a session dedicated to the introductory mindfulness practices. If a person recognizes that they are obsessing in some way in a particular meditative practice, they may choose to purposefully let go of that practice for awhile and change focus. In physical exercise, variety may be needed to prevent "repetitive stress fatigue." The same may be true of meditative practice.

Since Christian Tantric Meditation stages build upon each other, it is possible for a person go through an abbreviated version of early stages as they move into later stages. For example, a person might dwell for a short time working through the self emptying process, and then dwell for a short time in Divine Communion prior to practicing a more extended compassion meditation form. Consequently, a 20 minute self emptying exercise might evolve into a 30 to 40 minute compassion exercise.

Even people experienced with meditation have days where they find it difficult to stabilize and quiet their minds. On days like these, practicing only simple mindful breathing for 20 minutes can be very restorative and helpful. Once a stabilized mind is restored, the practice of Christian Tantric Meditation stages can be resumed.

If a person finds that on some days they just don't have the time for a full practice, they may choose to engage in an abbreviated single stage exercise as needed.

Once a person gets comfortable with the practice, it is possible to engage in stages of practice while sitting in a waiting room or during an airplane flight. Moving through the chakras with the specific intent of self emptying, Divine Communion, and focused compassion can become a source of comfort, like a rosary practice in the Catholic faith.

It can be useful to use a smartphone application like "ZaZen Meditation Timer." With such an application, a person can program a series of "gongs" to help guide their pace. One possible approach is to program a single, double, triple, double, and finally a single gong at 4 to 6 minute intervals, ensuring a total meditation time between 20 to 30 minutes per session

Whether a person chooses to practice every day, every other day, or 3 times per week, it is recommended that a person try to rotate through the practices to maintain a sense of balance. A rotating meditation discipline might look something like this:

Day 1: Simple Mindful Breathing (20 minutes total)

Day 3: Abbreviated Mindful Breathing(AMB) (4 minutes) plus Self Emptying (SE) Meditation (20 minutes, 24 minutes total)

Day 5: AMB (2 minutes), Abbreviated SE (4 minutes) plus Divine Communion Meditation (DCM) (20 minutes, 26 minutes total)

Day 7: ASE (4 minutes), Abbreviated DCM (4 minutes), and Compassion for Self (20 minutes, 28 minutes total)

Day 9: ASE, ADCM, and Compassion for Loved One or Companion Group

Day 11: ASE, ADCM, and Compassion for Hostile person or group

Day 13: ASE, ADCM, and Universal Compassion

With regard to balance in life overall, as self awareness grows, a person may choose to build in areas that have been neglected in the past. For example, a naturally introspective person who is drawn to meditation may choose to dedicate some disciplined effort towards socializing. Joining a church or taking a class, or spending time with family and friends may be areas of applying some discipline.

Likewise, a naturally social person may choose to dedicate disciplined effort towards becoming more comfortable with reflecting on her/his thoughts and feelings. Walking in nature, praying, or reading may be areas where one can engage in self reflection.

Self awareness regarding physical health may grow as well. A person may be inspired to engage in a disciplined physical activity, with more attention being paid to nutritional and sleep needs.

A person who recognizes they have a predisposition toward overly ambitious, overly pessimistic, or highly emotional thinking may choose to dedicate discipline toward balancing their thinking, and may dedicate meditation time developing that balance as well.

A person who begins to recognize they are in one or more unhealthy relationships may begin to exercise healthy boundaries.

As we assimilate the various stages of Christian Tantric Meditation into our lives, we also develop a meditative discipline that helps us to achieve balance. The integration of meditation practice and balance in day to day thinking and behaviors can help increase one's capacity for mindfulness, love, self confidence, and compassion.

TANTRIC PRACTICE AND CHRISTIAN TRADITION

The path that is followed in Christian Tantric Meditation very much parallels the path that Christ took in his life and ministry. Christians may recall the story of Christ wandering in the wilderness for 40 days. This part of Christ's Divine Journey is reminiscent of the practice of self emptying. During this time Jesus released His human desires to the extent that He was not vulnerable to temptation. Similarly, in Christian Tantric Meditation, we release our desires, our resentments, and our fears that hold us back and prevent us from receiving and accepting the Divine nature that is a part of who we are.

Wandering in the wilderness also prepared Jesus to accept the gift of the Holy Spirit that was to come. Remember that as Jesus received the gift of the Holy Spirit, the voice of God the Divine Parent reminded us of Christ's true nature – beloved Child of God, human and Divine. This part of Jesus' journey is paralleled in the Christian tantric process of Divine Communion, accepting and acknowledging the Divine Nature that is a part of who we are as people. As Parent God declared God's love for Jesus and acknowledged Jesus the Child's human and Divine nature, so too we accept the healing Grace that reminds us how much we are loved and how we also are children of the Divine parent. And as God's children, we acknowledge and accept our own Divine nature as well. Just as Jesus demonstrated, we too are human and Divine.

One might think that after enduring such emptiness and then enjoying such Divine Grace, Jesus might have found a tree to sit under

89

next to a stream and simply existed in a state of Bliss, in eternal Communion with God the parent. But that was not the path that Jesus took. From the moment of Jesus' Divine revelation, Jesus turned to His human brothers and sisters, conveying His blessings of healing and hope and love upon the rest of humanity. So too progresses Christian Tantric Meditation. After participating in Divine Communion, the Christian tantric method turns our compassion outward towards humanity, conveying our compassion to others.

Even during Christ's experience of the Easter Passion, a similar process was repeated. In an act of ultimate sacrifice, Jesus emptied Himself completely, offering his body as a sacrifice on behalf of humanity. He then experienced the ultimate Divine Communion, being taken up in Spirit and embracing His Divine Nature. And then, on Easter Sunday, Jesus returned to offer God's comfort and healing Grace to those who remained behind in mourning.

Not only Jesus, but the disciples as well entered into a similar journey. With the crucifixion of Jesus, they experienced self emptying, after which during Pentecost they received the Gift of Communion with the Holy Spirit. After the Pentecost experience, the disciples turned their focus outward towards people seeking help, and built the Christian Church.

The story is repeated over and over again with all the saints and enlightened ones the world has known. The apostle Paul experienced self emptying on the road to Damascus, followed by Communion with Christ and an outward turning to help others. St. Francis of Assisi had a similar story, as have many others.

The journeys of sainted women are also similar. Ruth garnered wheat stubble in self emptied poverty, and found redemption and shared her gifts with others. Mary wandered in the wilderness and received the gift of the Holy Spirit, and shared that gift, her beloved child Jesus, with the world. Mary Magdalene, and Mary and Martha of Bethany all shared similar experiences, as have sainted women ever since, including Claire and Theresa of Avila.

If we look at other cultures, the story is repeated again and again as well for revered sages. Buddha entered a period of wandering in the wilderness and experienced self emptying, after which he received a gift of enlightenment and turned his attentions to sharing the gifts he received, the Dharma, with others.

Thus, this tantric process of self emptying, Divine communion, and outward compassion is very much in harmony with Christian scripture and experience. For Christians who desire to walk in Christ's path, Christian Tantric Meditation offers an opportunity to do just that.

Tantric Meditation, Repentance, and 12 Step Practice

The tantric meditation process follows not only the path that Christ and the Saints have forged, but also the traditional path of repentance.

The traditional path of repentance includes "churchy" words like confession, contrition, penance, and reconciliation. While the traditional repentance model is often criticized for being judgmental and punishing, judgment and punishment need not be part of the process. Taken with unconditional love and healing in mind, Christian Tantric Meditation and traditional repentance follow similar paths. The repentance process has been used for millennia as a method for bringing about reconciliation and healing.

The Christian Tantric process of self emptying literally embodies the act of confession in the presence of the Holy Spirit. Similarly, the process of Divine Communion involves accepting Christ into our hearts, which brings about healing and reconciliation. The process of accepting Christ into our hearts also embodies the traditional acceptance of Salvation.

Finally, the process of compassion meditation works as a form of penance in bringing healing and reconciliation with others. As an act of penance, compassion meditation flows forth in loving response rather than as punishing obligation.

Similarly, the 12 Step Recovery process follows the long established repentance tradition. Values such as recognizing addiction as a problem, surrendering self care to a Higher Power, being willing to accept healing, and making amends where possible all have much in common with the mindfulness, self emptying, Divine Communion, and compassion processes that comprise Christian Tantric Meditation.

In traditional repentant practice, prayer and reflection leads to specific actions such as abstinence and rebuilding damaged relationships. Christian tantric meditation acts as a form of prayer that emphasizes listening and relationship with one's Higher Power, which also naturally leads to restorative healing actions for self and others.

CONCLUSION

The introduction to the Christian Tantric Meditation process asked us to visualize ourselves in an open field on a starry night. We were asked to imagine being able to empty ourselves of our daily distractions to completely experience the wonder of the scene. We were also asked to imagine recognizing the presence of a Divine Creator, and the Divinity that is a part of who we are as Beings created in the image of the God. We were also asked to recognize and have compassion for all living beings that share this world and this universe with us. Finally, we were asked to recognize who we are as whole, complete beings – as transparent Spirit, as glowing Divine , and as living humans, made in the image of God, living in connected nonduality with God and with all of creation.

The process we imagined in the introduction of this text provided a fair representation of what Christian Tantric Meditation entails and tries to achieve. May we all recognize the hopeful and joyful presence of God, the Loving presence of Christ, the Wise and Faithful presence of God as Mary-Sophia, and the Holy Spirit that brings life and binds us all in nondual Communion with Creator and all of Creation.

Christian Tantric Meditation can have the effects of reducing stress, increasing self esteem, and increasing empathy and compassion. Meditative practice can also have the effects of reducing stress, and promoting physical and psychological healing.

Amen.

93

David J. Miller

TESTIMONIAL: THE AUTHOR'S MEDITATIVE JOURNEY

The path that led to the creation of this book had many twists and turns along the way, but has been very rewarding.

The journey began with a prophetic experience followed by a medical emergency. During the prophetic experience in April of 1994 I became aware of my calling to help people who endure suffering. In November of that year an accumulation of scar tissue in my trachea led to a complete closure of my airway, which resulted in losing my ability to talk. One might say I was forced into a vow of silence. I was also forced into a lifestyle centered on listening.

The resultant process of reconstructive surgeries took several years, during which I remained without a voice. I was able to use a buzzer held to my throat to communicate with, but that was uncomfortable and hard to understand.

I began writing about the feelings I was processing and about my relationship with God. David L Davis, an ordained pastor friend of mine, read through my writings and suggested that I obtain the theological language I needed to better express myself by attending Divinity School. I entered the Master's of Theological Studies program at Emory University in 1996.

During my time at Emory, I attended a class called Contextual Education. In that class I helped minister to homeless people in the Atlanta Union Mission's men's recovery program. As I still had no voice, I was forced to "just listen" to the people I worked with, offering

94

no advice whatever. I was blessed to witness not only the amazing stories and wonderful cultural diversity of the people I worked with, but also the miraculous healing properties that empathetic listening can provide.

During that time I also came upon the book "Prayer" by Richard Foster, which I talk about in the text of this book. (Foster, 1992). His chapter on meditative prayer as a "listening prayer" moved me, and became a part of my personal prayer discipline.

I shared the prayer and meditative practices that I engaged in with the men in the AUM recovery program while teaching Spirituality classes there. I taught classes over a course of 9 years, long after the Contextual Education class at Emory ended and I had received my Master's degree in Theological Studies.

While engaging in theologically oriented discussion groups, I met Bruce Alderman, who became a very good friend over the years. Bruce had spent several years traveling throughout Asia and studying Buddhist practices. He currently serves as an adjunct instructor in Consciousness and Transformative Studies at John F. Kennedy University in the San Francisco Bay area. Bruce is an excellent Integral scholar and very engaging in theological and philosophical discussions. This text would not have been possible without his encouragement and generous sharing of his studies and experience in tantric practice.

When asked questions about Buddhist perspectives on theological subjects, Bruce was an engaging dialog partner, and often recommended books for me to read.   He directed me towards both Christian contemplative and Buddhist scholars, including Thomas Keating, and Tarthang Tulku.

By this time, I had started working towards a Master's Degree in Community Counseling at Argosy University in Atlanta. Mindfulness was a popular "buzz" word at the time in psychological circles, and I chose to focus my counseling orientation in that direction.

I began to practice meditation in a manner consistent with the writings of Thich Nhat Hanh, focusing on breathing and developing a sense of mindfulness. This practice in combination with my prayerful meditative practices continued for several years.

At some point I began reading books on Tantric Meditation, including the "Six Yogas of Naropa" by Tsong Kha Pa. (Mullen, 1996) Tsong Kha Pa was a Tibetan scholar living about 600 years ago. I began incorporating portions of the "Six Yoga" practice into my meditative discipline as well.

I also read "Introduction to Tantra" by Lama Yeshe (Yeshe, 2001), and other works as well, which helped enlighten me to the practices of Guru Yoga and Compassion Meditation.

Having received my Master's in Community Counseling, I began working in addiction recovery programs professionally. I also shared my meditative practice learnings with clients. While investigating meditative techniques for helping chronic pain patients, I came across the books "Dissolving Pain" (Fehmi, 2007) and "Open Focused Brain" (Fehmi, 2010) by Les Fehmi. I began using the techniques described in "Dissolving Pain" personally and professionally, and I personally found relief from long standing physical pain issues.

As I read through "Dissolving Pain" and "Open Focused Brain" I also recognized harmonies between the practices Fehmi described and Buddhist tantric meditative practices. I later discovered that "Open Focus" practices were very much in harmony with practices described by Tarthang Tulku in "Time, Space and Knowledge." (Tulku, 1977.) I also recognized harmonies between Buddhist practices, 12 step recovery programs, and Christian repentance traditions.

At some point I began participating in spiritual direction with Rev. Lou Kava PhD. Lou's multi-disciplined expertise in Christian contemplative and mindfulness meditation practice, Spirituality, and psychology provided a much needed sounding board and direction in the midst of all the ideas that culminated in this text. Lou's gentle and persistent admonition to "stay in the here and now" has played an important role in this text and in my personal meditative practice.

Lou also recommended that I participate in Cognitive Behavioral Compassion Meditative training offered through Emory University. The class, instructed by Geshe Lobsang Tenzin Negi PhD, helped me to recognize that my approach to meditation and especially compassion was one sided, leaning towards recognizing only the "pathological" aspects of the human condition. Geshe helped me to see the aspirational aspect of compassion, recognizing not only common suffering but also common aspirations that are part of the human experience.

The meditative process described in this text has been very liberating for me personally. Like many people, I carried and continue to carry lingering desires, long term resentments, and long standing fears. The process described here has helped me to become more accepting and loving of myself and others. It has also helped me to become a more tolerant and peaceful human being.

As a therapist, the practice of self emptying has been invaluable. When a client opens her/his self up to a therapist, the therapist needs to immerse her/himself into the worldview of the client. This immersion naturally fosters compassion, and compassion fosters healing.

While practicing "self emptying," I personally experienced what John of the Cross called the "Dark Night of the Soul." Much of the insight I share regarding maintaining transparency to help fill the gap left by the surrender of fears and resentments stem from my own experience. I was fortunate to be engaged in both Spiritual Direction with Lou Kavar and Professional Supervision with Kim Waters Rose LPC as I worked through that phase of my development.

The practice of "Communing with Divinity" has been invaluable as well. My self confidence, self esteem, and sense of empowerment have increased along with my capacity to forgive myself and others and love unconditionally. My personal relationship with Jesus Christ has become deeper and more meaningful as well.

Psychological and theological training all motivated me to emphasize humility in the sense of "remaining grounded" as part of this practice. The human mind is so creative and wonderful that it can be swept into "other-worldly" expectations in unhealthy ways. Historical heresies dismissing the humanity of Christ and practitioners, and various cult occurrences both historical and recent attest to potential tragic results arising from unhealthy other-worldly expectations. Remaining grounded throughout this practice is essential.

The fact that unhealthy other-worldly expectations are possible does not, however, diminish the role of mystical experience in communing with God through Christ. Profoundly moving mystical experiences are often encountered in a wide variety of settings, within and outside of meditation. The test I apply as to whether or not a "mystical" experience is genuine and "healthy" is found in Galatians 5:22. If the experience bears the fruits of love, peace, patience, kindness, faithfulness, gentleness, and self control, it is safe to say that the Spirit has been present in the experience.

I personally have encountered many profoundly moving experiences during meditation, all of which have contributed to the development of this Christian Tantric Meditation practice. I have experienced Communion of Saints, Communion with Christ, and a sense of reconciling wholeness. I have also found great joy and relief in practicing compassion meditation with both "loving" and "hostile" relationships in mind.

As a counselor I have worked with a great may clients engaged in serious and sometimes dangerous codependent relationships. Hence the emphasis on boundaries, acceptance, and respect. We can only hope to change ourselves, and changing ourselves in positive ways often improves our relationships.

Along with traditional cognitive behavioral education and treatment, meditative practice can be a powerful tool in dealing with the disease of addiction and other mental health issues. As mentioned in this text, meditation practice can aid in the treatment of addiction, depression, anxiety, control issues, and codependent relationship issues. That said, if you or someone you love is struggling with one or more of these issues, it is highly recommended that you engage professional treatment. As a supplement to professional treatment, the use of meditative practice, whether it is prayer oriented, mindfulness oriented, or in keeping with the practices described in this text, can do a great deal to help a person learn about themselves and the challenges they face.

Dave Miller

June 2014

REFERENCES

Advertisement (1976, March-April). Nyingma Institute Seminar. *Yoga Journal, Volume* II #2, p. 19

Fehmi, Les and Robbins, Jim (2010) Dissolving Pain: Simple Brain-Training Exercises for Overcoming Pain. Boston, Ma: Trumpeter Books

Fehmi, Les and Robbins, Jim (2007) The Open Focus Brain: Harnessing the Power of Attention to Heal Mind and Body . Boston, Ma.: Trumpeter Books

Foster, Richard J. (1992) Prayer: Finding the Heart's True Home. New York, NY.: Harper Collins

Hahn, Thich Nhat (1975) The Miracle of Mindfulness Boston, Ma.: Beacon Press

Hahn, Thich Nhat (2010) Reconciliation: Healing the Inner Child. Berkely, Ca: Parallax Press

Kohn, Sherab Chodzin (2011) A Life of the Buddha. Boston, Ma.: Shambhala Publications.

Ladner, Lorne (2004) The Lost Art of Compassion: Discovering the Practice of Happiness in the Meeting of Buddhism and Psychology. New York, NY: Harper Collins

McLeod, S. A. (2007). Maslow's Hierarchy of Needs. Retrieved from http://www.simplypsychology.org/maslow.html

Mullin, Glen H. (1996) The Six Yogas of Naropa. Ithaca, New York: Snow Lion Publications

Negi, Geshe Lobsang Tenzin (2014) Cognitive Based Compassion Training. www.tibet.emory.edu/cbct/#CBCT

Padmakara Translation Group (2006) The Way of the Boddhisattva. Boston, Ma.: Shambhala Publications.

Tulku, Tarthang (1977) Time, Space, and Knowledge. Berkely, Ca.:Dharma Publishing.

Wallis, Christopher (2012) Tantra Illuminated. Petaluma, Ca.: Mattamayura Press.

Yeshe, Thubton, Lama (2001) Introduction to Tantra : The Transformation of Desire. Somerville, Ma.: Wisdom Publications.

ABOUT THE AUTHOR

Dave Miller has earned a Master's in Community Counseling from Argosy University Atlanta Georgia, a Master's in Theological Studies from Emory University in Atlanta Georgia, and a Bachelor's of Science in Electrical Engineering from Milwaukee School of Engineering in Milwaukee Wisconsin. As a Lay Minister and as a Licensed Associate Professional Counselor, Dave has worked in Recovery, Mental Health, Judicial, and Church settings.

Dave has been studying and practicing various forms of meditation for decades. Dave began by practicing a form of "listening prayer" in combination with "Lectio Divina" reading of Psalms and Christ's Gospels. Since then, Dave has studied and practiced mindfulness, self emptying, Guru Yoga, and compassion meditation techniques. His training in Psychology and Christian Theology, combined with his studies in tantric meditation, all contribute to his development of this powerful and unique Christian Tantric Meditation Practice. To learn more about Dave's counseling practice and Christian Tantric Meditation workshops, visit www.EcumenicalWellness.org.

Made in the USA
Charleston, SC
27 August 2014